Index to Projects

W9-CPV-007

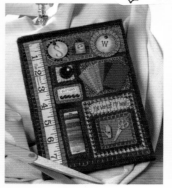

Basic Supplies

Fabric, wool, felt, thread, floss, needle

Buttons, bottle caps, accents

Bottle Caps

Flatten Caps:
To flute the edges, place a cap on scrap wood then hit the cap a few times with a rubber mallet.

Or flatten caps in a Sizzix® die-cut machine by adding 2 marble tiles.

Bottle Caps are available from Design Originals www.d-originals.com

Shepard's Cup Journal Cover

Good to the last page, this java journal cover will please the coffee lover in your family as much as their morning brew. When the pages are used up, simply remove the journal cover and insert a new notebook!
instructions & patterns on pages 22 - 25

Tips from the Artist

I have listed the materials I used to make each project, but I encourage you to substitute items that you have on hand. Also, to make your work personally significant, I recommend that you use fabrics that belonged to the person who will receive the artwork whenever possible.

★ I used mostly wools for the quilted center, and a homespun or wool fabric for the book cover. Feel free to use what you would like.

★ When transferring shapes and words, use an "iron on transfer pencil", or write and draw shapes and words with a sharp pencil.

★ I have used several different accessories from *EK Success* Jolee's By You. I hope you will supplement these with your own handmade accessories.

★ Use fabric glue to adhere fabrics, use glue stick on paper. E6000 will adhere metal charms and bottle caps to paper and fabric.

★ I recommend and use The Warm Company's Steam-A-Seam II fusible web. When tracing a pattern onto Steam-A-Seam II, be sure to trace the wrong side of the pattern. A light table is useful for transferring patterns to Steam-A-Seam II.

★ You can alter brads with paint or a marker.

★ Dictionary definitions have been provided for you to copy onto cardstock. You can also computer print the desired words on cardstock or Muslin, or cut up a dictionary from the second-hand book store.

★ If you cannot find the scrapbook papers you want, find graphics in books and magazines or print images from the internet onto your own papers. All projects use a quarter inch seam allowance.

★ I used 2 strands of floss for embroidering the larger pieces and words, and one strand for smaller pieces.

'Sew' Journal

Show off your love of hand work and sewing with the journal. It's perfect for taking notes at sewing class, collecting the photos and notes about completed projects, or outlining ideas for future projects. This journal is a lovely gift for anyone who loves to sew.

instructions and patterns on pages 38 - 39

Small Purses

Display your collection of sewing memorabilia in a wearable, take-along format. Your friends will definitely want a closer look when you show up at the next sewing circle or embroidery guild meeting carrying your scissors, thimble and needles in this little purse. These purses provide the ultimate canvas for art that honors your heartfelt homemade hobby.

instructions and patterns on pages 26 - 27

I Love Ewe

Soft as a fluffy lamb, this wool book cover offers a sweet sentiment.

instructions and patterns on pages 28 - 30

Hearts Journal

Collect your love notes in a truly heartfelt journal. This pretty design is going to inspire the cupid in all of us. Record your favorite poetry and loving thoughts in this beautiful book.

instructions and patterns on pages 32 - 33

Valentine Purse

Remember how great it felt to give out Valentines at school? Pack this purse with happy notes to share with friends and co-workers and you will bring a smile to everyone you meet.

instructions and patterns on page 31

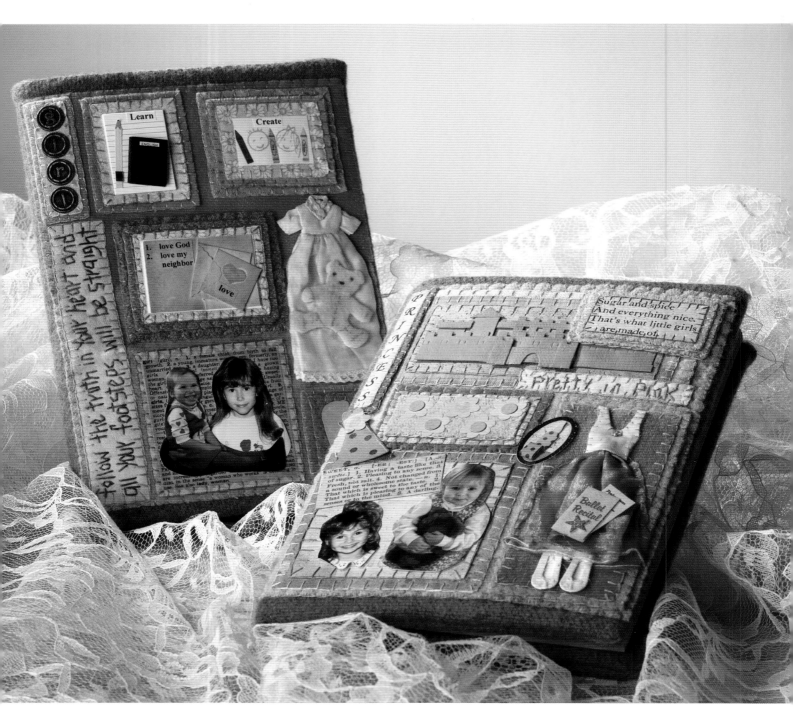

Pretty in Pink

I designed this book for my "Princess". Every child is unique, and this one was my very feminine little lady. She was the one who always wore pink. I hope this design gives you some ideas for expressing your child's individual personality.

instructions and patterns on pages 34 - 35

Christina's Journal

Christina is my writer. Making a journal for her seemed so appropriate. She has been writing stories since she was very young. I chose embellishments that have very special and private meanings for her. She has grown into a very loving and generous spirit. I am very proud of her.

instructions and patterns on pages 36 - 37

Boy's Journal

*Trains and planes and teddy bears,
'Twas a time I had no cares.
Soccer shoes, baseball caps and football,
I hold the memories of them all.
    Make a journal your sons will treasure using embell-
ishments that are "all boy".*

instructions and patterns on pages 40 - 41

as you grow the fingerprints of who you are will remain the same

Stockings Journal

I love children's books, especially those by Dr. Seuss. I wanted to decorate this book with things that are fun. The striped sock reminds me of the hat worn by the Cat in the Hat, and the words bring to mind many of the stories by that famous author.

I added "the stockings were hung" to give this book a coordinated theme. Nothing goes together like Christmas, children's stories and fun.

instructions and patterns on pages 42 - 43

Multiply Journal

Remember the alphabet samplers traditionally taught so we could practice our embroidered letters? Well, I love math and numbers and this is a great way to practice stitching. I also thought this would be a fun book for someone who can't remember their multiplication tables, or for a child who is just learning them. It's also a nice present for your child's math teacher.

instructions and patterns on pages 44 - 45

Games People Play Journal

My family loves games. Old games, new games, puzzles, we play them all. I almost wish the journal were bigger so I could include more of our favorites. I hope you will cover your book with the games you love best.

instructions and patterns on pages 45 - 47

Framed Seed Art

Mary, Mary, quite contrary, how does your garden grow?
From many seed packets, all planted in a row!

   Seed packet art reproductions are available in a variety of media, from paper to fabric. This is my rendition of that tradition. Each seed packet has been sewn in place and the entire work displayed in an old wooden frame. If you can't find an old frame, scuff up a new one with a bit of sandpaper.
   I encourage you to use this design as a starting point for creating seed packets of your favorite plants.
   There is always time for planting and harvest. I hope you take the time to enjoy making this garden of art so you can reap the pleasures of seeing your finished work hanging in your home.
   Remember, you can always make a smaller frame with fewer packets if you prefer a smaller project.

instructions and patterns on pages 49 - 53

Seeds Purse

   Keep your list of seeds and your garden plans in this handy purse and you will always be ready for that spur-of-the-moment decision to stop at the nursery on the way home from work.
   Easy embellishments make this purse a fun choice to sew on a quiet afternoon.

instructions and patterns on page 48

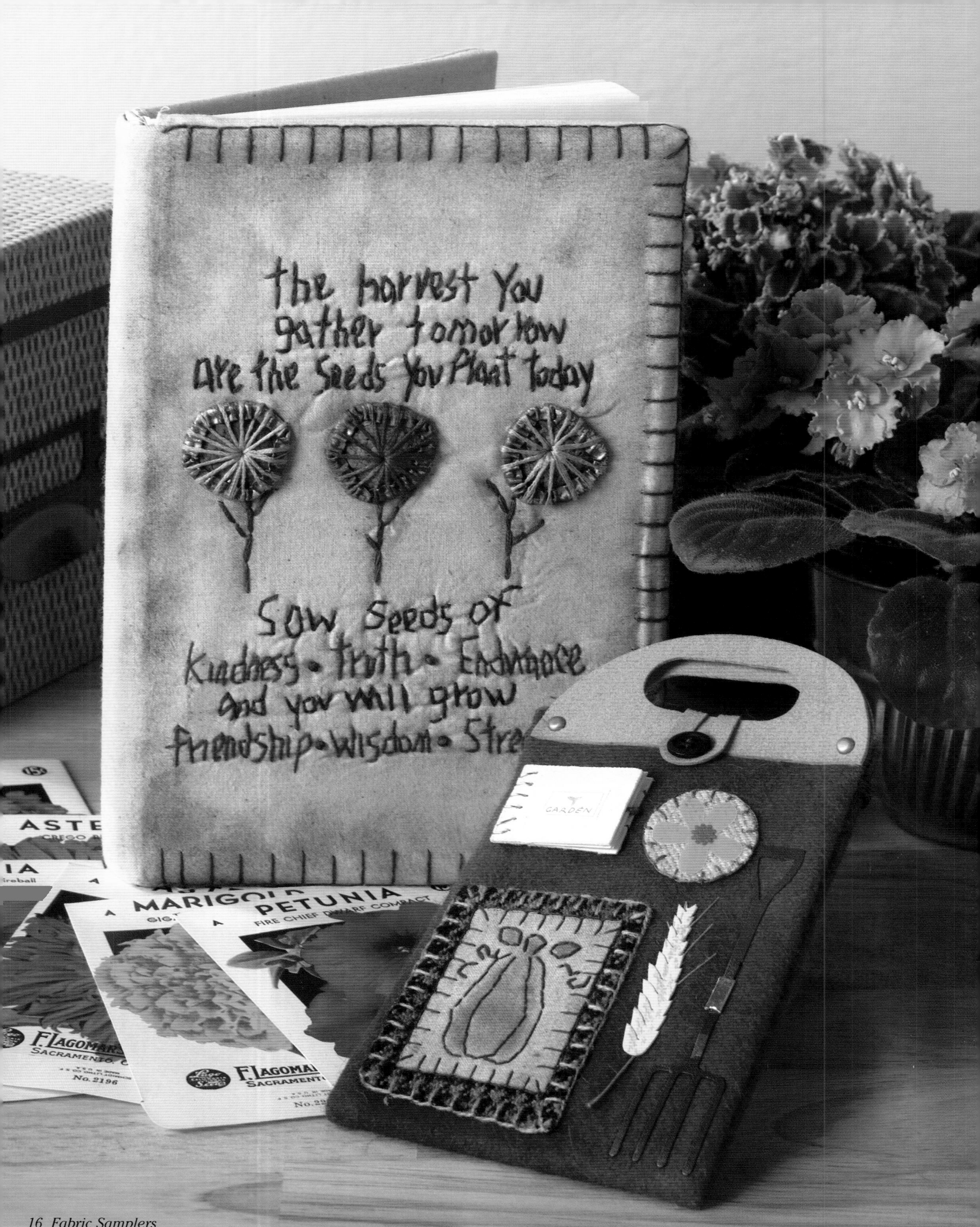

the harvest You
gather tomorrow
are the Seeds You Plant Today

Sow Seeds of
Kindness • Truth • Endurance
and you will grow
Friendship • Wisdom • Stre

Harvest Journal

The harvest you gather tomorrow are the seeds you plant today. If you want a happy future, plant good deeds now. Sow a little extra kindness into your days today and you will reap friends forever.

This is one of the easiest journal covers of all. The flower embellishments are made by flattening a bottle cap around a button and then adding floss. The titles are simple backstitch.

instructions and patterns on page 56

Pumpkin Purse

Autumn is one of my favorite times of the year. It is a time to celebrate the bounty of the earth and give thanks for a plentiful harvest. This purse uses some of my favorite motifs of the season.

instructions and patterns on page 54

Pumpkin Harvest Journal

Every gardener will enjoy this journal with its rich colors and symbols of harvest time.

Record all of your favorite harvest time recipes in this book and give it to a friend for Thanksgiving, or create a family keepsake by transcribing Grandma's recipes into this book and sharing it with members of the family.

instructions and patterns on pages 54 - 55

Garden Blooms Wall Hanging

Home is where my flowers grow. What a beautiful sentiment! Show off this welcoming art on your front porch or in the sunroom to proclaim your love of growing things.

instructions and patterns on pages 57 - 59

Journal Covers

GENERAL MATERIALS:
5½" x 8½" journal • 9" x 23" fabric for cover

GENERAL INSTRUCTIONS:
Make the decorated piece for the desired project.
See individual project for the color of wool and cut 1 book cover 9" x 23".
Study the diagrams on this page.
Place the wrong side of fabric against the table.

Making the Soft Book Cover

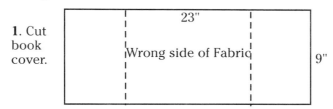

1. Cut book cover.

23"
Wrong side of Fabric
9"

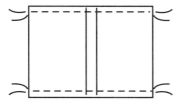

3. Sew across long ends. Trim threads and turn cover right side out.

End View of Book

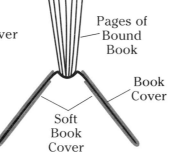

Pages of Bound Book

Book Cover

Soft Book Cover

4. Slide the soft cover onto the bound book.

Fold each end in 5½", leaving a 1" opening in the center.
Sew across the long sides.
Turn the cover right side out.
Position and fuse the decorated piece to the journal cover.
Blanket stitch all around the edge of the decorated piece. See individual project for floss color.
Holding the pages of the book together, let the front and back covers hang down. This will allow you to easily slide the book covers into the pockets of the journal cover.

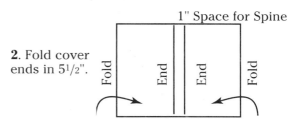

1" Space for Spine

2. Fold cover ends in 5½".

Fold | End | End | Fold

Note: All projects use a 1/4" seam allowance.
Use 2 strands of floss for larger pieces and Backstitching words.
Use 1 strand for smaller pieces.

Flower Pincushion

Unique pincushions are a collectible art form. Make this one to add to your collection or give it as a gift for the seamstress in your family. It's a pretty decoration for the sewing room or dressing table.

instructions and patterns on pages 59 - 61

General Instructions for Using Steam-A-Seam II

Steam-A-Seam II is a permanent bonding fusible web when applied correctly.

1. Wash, dry and press cotton fabric to remove the sizing so the fusible web will permanently adhere.

2. Steam-A-Seam II has paper on 2 sides. Using a light table, trace the applique pattern in reverse with a pencil, on the top side of the quick fuse paper backing.

3. Peel the paper backing off the other side and finger press the web to the wrong side of your fabric. Cut out the applique shapes.

4. Peel off the backing and position the pieces as desired.

5. Press in place for 12-20 seconds following the manufacturer's directions.

Purse

GENERAL MATERIALS:
4" square heavy fabric, leather, or suede • 4¼" x 10½" purse fabric • Button • Two ¼" brads • 1 yard cording or jute • Large eye needle • Steam-A-Seam II

GENERAL INSTRUCTIONS:

Handle:
1. From heavy fabric, leather, or suede, cut out 1 Handle Pattern on fold. See Diagram 1.
2. Cut the circle into 2 semicircles on the fold. See Diagram 2.
3. Draw the center hole for the handle on both semicircles. See Diagram 3.
4. Fold each semicircle in half. Doing so makes it easier to cut out the center hole. See Diagram 4.
5. One of the pieces you cut out will be used to make the Closure Strap. Cut a hole out of the center. See Diagram 5.
6. Press ¼" strip of Steam-A-Seam II to bottom of purse handles. See Diagram 6.

Purse body:
7. Cut Purse fabric 4" x 10½".

8. Embroider as desired, keeping the design away from the ¼" seam lines.
9. Fold purse body in half with right sides together, sew side seams. See Diagram 7.
10. Turn right side out. Press flat.
11. Press each handle to top edges of the front and back of the purse.
12. Tack stitch the Closure Strap to back of purse.
13. Pull Closure strap through handle to front.
14. Sew a button that the strap will fit over to the front of the purse. See Diagram 8.

Purse string:
15. Knot 1 end of the cording and thread the other end through a needle.
16. Poke the needle from the inside of one side of the purse, pulling the knot against the inside of the purse.
17. Poke the needle from the outside of the purse to the inside. Tie a knot to secure the purse string.
18. Make 2 small holes with a large eye needle, through the sides of the handle. Put a brad into each hole. See Diagram 9.

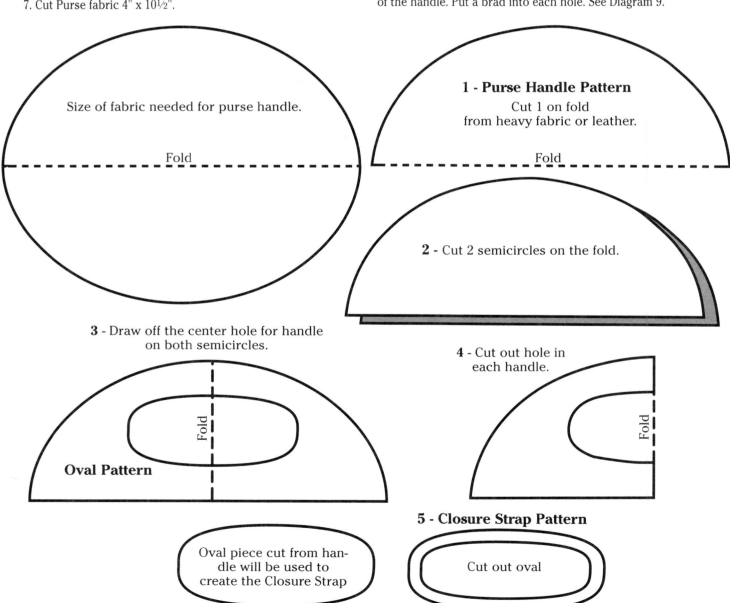

Size of fabric needed for purse handle.

Fold

1 - Purse Handle Pattern
Cut 1 on fold
from heavy fabric or leather.

Fold

2 - Cut 2 semicircles on the fold.

3 - Draw off the center hole for handle on both semicircles.

Fold

Oval Pattern

4 - Cut out hole in each handle.

Fold

Oval piece cut from handle will be used to create the Closure Strap

5 - Closure Strap Pattern

Cut out oval

_ _ _ _ Handle Placement _ _ _ _

Seam

7 - Purse Body Pattern

Cut 1 from Heavy Fabric,
Leather or Suede

Place on fold of Fabric

6 - Press Steam-A-Seam ll to bottom of each
purse handle.

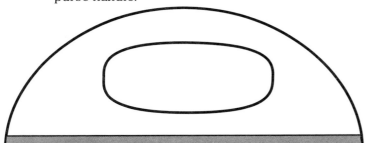

8 & 9 - The finished handle (shown actual
size) with strap brads and button closure.

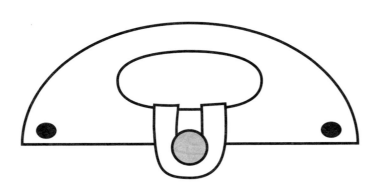

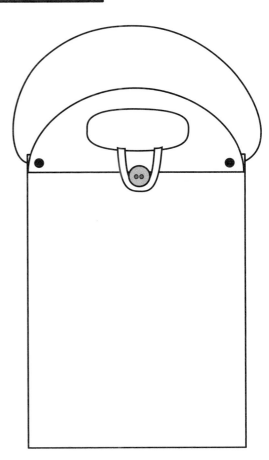

Shepard's Cup Cafe Journal

MATERIALS:

Wool (9" x 23" Light Green cover, 5¾" x 8¼" Dark Green Background for #1, 1¼" x 5¾" Black Green Houndstooth for #2; 1¼" x 7" Light Green Plaid for #3, 1½" x 4¼" Tan Tweed for #4, 2" x 3½" Purple for #5, 1½" x 3½" Rust for #6) • Muslin (2" x 3¼" for Warm Words, ½" x 4¾" for Welcome #3, 1¼" x 1⅝" for Full Cup, ¾" x 2½" for Here to Serve) • Wool Appliques (**For Shepard's Cup**: 2¼" x 3½" Black/Tan Houndstooth, 2⅝" x 3⅞" Gold; **For Welcome #3**: 1½" square Black/Tan Houndstooth, ¾" x 5¾" Red; **For Hand block**: 2" White; **For Spoon block**: 1¾" x 3¼" Lavender, 1" x 3" Green; **For Coffee block**: 1¼" x 4" Rose and 2" scraps of Black/Green Houndstooth, Gold, Purple for tags) • Charms (Gold spoon, Silver coffee cup) • ⅛" brads (4 Brass, 3 Black) • *ColorBox* Light Rose ink • *DMC* floss (Tan, Green, Black, Brown, Red, Light Green, Mauve, Dark Brown, Dark Green) • Needle • Thread • Steam-A-Seam II • Sponge

INSTRUCTIONS:

1. Cut out pieces #1-6 using the Wool Placement diagram on page 23. Apply Steam-A-Seam II to the back of all pieces. Fuse pieces #2-6 in place.
2. Blanket stitch #3 with Green floss, #4 with Tan floss, #5 with Light Green, and #6 with Tan.
3. Trace the reverse patterns of the hand and tags, including the Muslin squares and ovals onto Steam-A-Seam II. Press to fabrics. Cut out all the Appliques.
4. Fuse Muslin squares and ovals to the tags. Fuse the Hand in place on #6.

EMBROIDERY:

5. Backstitch words on hand with Black floss and the heart with Red floss.
6. Backstitch "COFFEE" on each tag, using French Knots in place of the dots. The "C" is Black, the "O" is Red, The first "F" is Green, the second "F" is Black, the "E" is Red, the last "E" is Green.
7. Transfer 4 patterns from page 25 to the Muslin.
8. Backstitch "Warm Words hot Coffee" and "Your cup is always full" with Red floss. Backstitch "Shepard's Cup Cafe" and the cof-fee cup with Brown floss. Backstitch the curly lines with Green. Satin stitch a Red heart. Cut out the reverse pattern for the candy cane from Steam-A-Seam II and press to Houndstooth. Fuse in place.
9. Welcome block: Backstitch "the door is narrow..." with Black floss.
10. Backstitch "here to serve" with Mauve floss.
11. Apply Steam-A-Seam II to all embroidered pieces. Cut out. Lightly apply Rose ink to "your cup is always full" and the hand with a sponge.

APPLIQUE:

12. **Shepard's Cup block**: Stack and fuse pieces to the Background. Blanket stitch around the Muslin and Houndstooth wool with Tan floss. Blanket stitch around the Gold wool with Brown floss.
13. **Welcome #3 block**: Cut out the reverse pattern for the Houndstooth from Steam-A-Seam II. Press all pieces in place on the Background. Blanket stitch around the Houndstooth and Muslin with Tan floss. Blanket stitch around the Red wool with Brown floss. Insert the brad through all layers.
14. **Hand block**: Fuse the Muslin in place. Blanket stitch around with Dark Brown.
15. **Here to Serve block**: Fuse the pieces to #5. Blanket stitch around the Muslin with Tan floss, around the Green wool with Dark Green floss, around the Lavender wool with Brown floss.
16. **Coffee block**: Fuse the tags to the Rose rectangle. Blanket stitch around the "C" tag with Tan floss, the "O" tag with Green floss, the Purple "F" with Mauve floss, the next "F" with Tan floss, the "E" with Green floss, and the last "E" with Mauve floss. Insert the brads, going through the Rose wool. Fuse Rose wool to Background #4. Blanket stitch around with Brown floss.
17. Make the book cover following the General Instructions on page 19.
18. Fuse Background to the book cover. Blanket stitch around Background with Brown floss.
19. Sew charms in place.

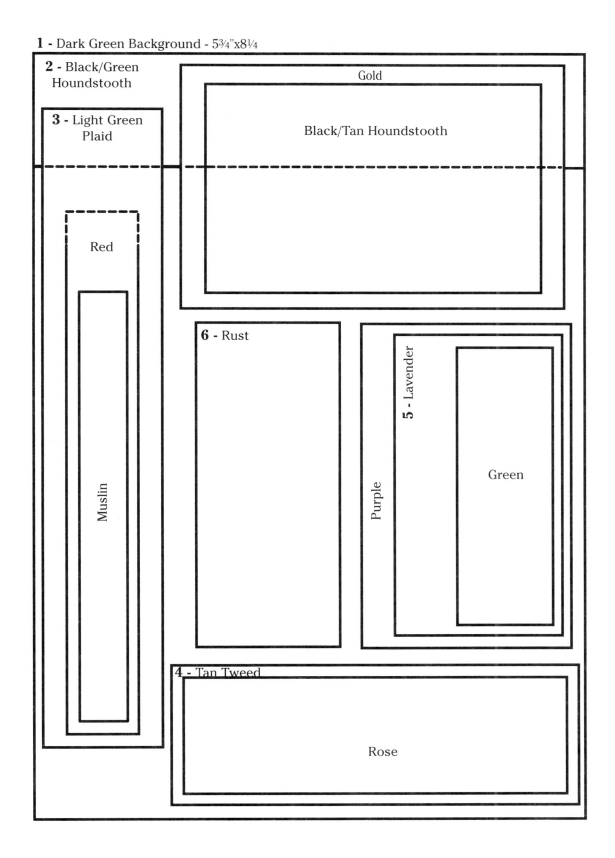

1 - Dark Green Background - 5¾"x8¼

2 - Black/Green Houndstooth

Gold

3 - Light Green Plaid

Black/Tan Houndstooth

Red

Muslin

6 - Rust

5 - Lavender

Purple

Green

4 - Tan Tweed

Rose

Shepard's Cup Placement Diagram Actual Size

1½" Square
Black/Tan Houndstooth

Welcome

Black
Houndstooth

Muslin

Muslin

the door is narrow, but all are Welcome

Hand
2" Square
Muslin

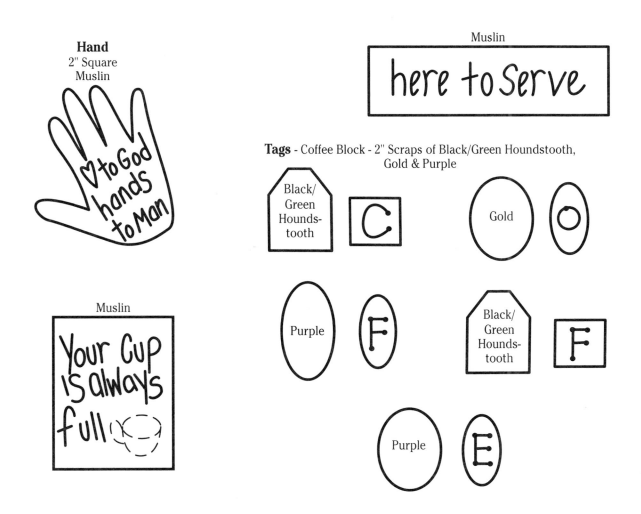

Muslin

here to Serve

Tags - Coffee Block - 2" Scraps of Black/Green Houndstooth,
Gold & Purple

Black/Green Houndstooth

C

Gold

O

Purple

F

Black/Green Houndstooth

F

Muslin

Your Cup is always full

Purple

E

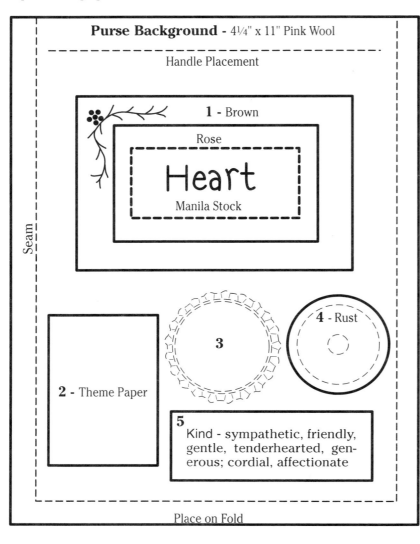

Purse Background - 4¼" x 11" Pink Wool

Handle Placement

1 - Brown

Rose

Heart

Manila Stock

Seam

2 - Theme Paper

3

4 - Rust

5
Kind - sympathetic, friendly, gentle, tenderhearted, generous; cordial, affectionate

Place on Fold

Heart Purse

MATERIALS:
Wool (4¼" x 11" Pink," 1⅞" x 2⅞" Brown, 1¼" x 2⅛" Rose, 1" circle Rust) • *Design Originals* (Silver bottle cap; Papers: #0549 Shorthand, #0500 TeaDye Keys) • Manila cardstock • 1⅛" x 1⅝" "sewing theme" paper • Silver coin • Cut out flower • Inkpad (Blue, Rose) • Red marker • *DMC* floss (Dark Brown, Tan, Light Brown, Dark Green, Rose, Mauve) • Needle • Thread • 1" circle punch • Small nail • Hammer • Rubber mallet • E6000

INSTRUCTIONS:
See General Instructions on page 20. Follow steps 1-8.

Block 1: Copy "Heart" pattern on Manila ¾" x 1¾" cardstock. Trace the letters with a Red marker. Smudge with Rose and Blue inks. • Blanket stitch cardstock to Rose wool with Light Brown floss. • Center Rose wool on Brown wool. Blanket stitch around the Rose wool with Tan floss. • In the corner of the Brown wool, Backstitch the vine with Dark Green floss. The flowers are made with Rose and Mauve French Knots. • Blanket stitch the Brown wool to the purse with Dark Brown floss.

Block 2: Blanket stitch the sewing theme paper in place.

Block 3: Flatten a bottle cap. Punch 2 small holes in the center. Sew the cap to the purses. • Punch a circle of TeaDye paper and glue it to the bottle cap. • Glue flower in place.

Block 4: Blanket stitch the Rust wool circle to the purse with Tan floss. • Glue the coin in place.

Block 5: Copy the definition of "Kind" on Manila cardstock. Cut it out to ¾" x 2⅛". Blanket stitch definition in place with Brown floss.

Continue with Step 9 of the General Instructions on page 20.

1 - Brown

2 - Theme Paper

Rust

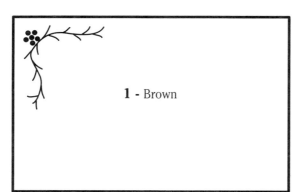

Rose

Heart

5 - Manila Stock

Kind- sympathetic, friendly, gentle, tenderhearted, generous; cordial, affectionate

Purse Background - 4¼" x 11" Green wool

Handle Placement

1

2 - Pink

Tape - ¼ x 1¼"

3 - Sewing Machine Ad

4 - Mini Floss

5 - Green

Seam

Place on Fold

Dress Form Purse

MATERIALS:
4¼" x 11" Green wool • *Design Originals* (Silver bottle cap; #0549 Shorthand paper) • *Jolee's By You* assorted embellishments • 2¼" x 3¼" Antique Sewing Machine ad • Pink button • *DMC* floss (Tan, Black) • Needle • Thread • 1" circle punch • Small nail • Hammer • Rubber mallet • E6000

INSTRUCTIONS:
See General Instructions on page 20. Follow steps 1-8.

Block 1: Flatten a bottle cap. Punch 2 holes in the center. Sew to purse. • Punch a circle of Shorthand paper and glue it to the bottle cap.

Block 2: Cut a Pink wool rectangle ⅝" x 2". Blanket stitch around with Tan floss. • Glue a mini ¼ x 1¼" measuring tape in place.

Block 3: Blanket stitch sewing machine ad in place with Tan floss. • Glue dress mannequin onto ad.

Block 4: Whipstitch the "5 mini floss" set in place.

Block 5: Cut Green wool rectangle ⅞" x 1⅛".
• Blanket stitch around rectangle with Black floss.
• Sew button in place.

Continue with Step 9 of the General Instructions on page 20.

Sewing Machine Purse

MATERIALS:
4¼" x 11" Pink wool • *Design Originals* (3 Silver bottle caps; Papers: #0549 Shorthand, #0500 TeaDye Keys) • *Jolee's By You* assorted embellishments • 2¼" x 2½" Antique Sewing Machine ad • 1⅜" x 1⅝" sewing theme paper • Chinese coin • *DMC* Tan floss • Needle • Thread • 1" circle punch • Small nail • Hammer • Rubber mallet • E6000

INSTRUCTIONS:
See General Instructions on page 20. Follow steps 1-8. Flatten 3 bottle caps. Punch 2 holes in the center of each cap. Sew to purse.

Block 1: Blanket stitch sewing machine ad in place with Tan floss. • Glue sewing machine onto ad.

Block 2: Punch a circle of Shorthand paper and glue it to the bottle cap. • Glue mini thread and needle in place.

Block 3: Punch a circle of Shorthand paper and glue it to the bottle cap. • Glue coin in place.

Block 4: Punch a circle of TeaDye paper and glue it to the bottle cap. • Glue mini scissors in place.

Block 5: Adhere small button card in place.

Block 6: Blanket stitch sewing theme paper in place with Tan floss.

Continue with Step 9 of the General Instructions shown on page 20.

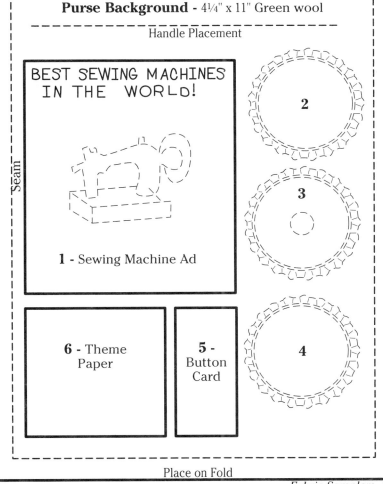

Purse Background - 4¼" x 11" Green wool

Handle Placement

BEST SEWING MACHINES
IN THE WORLD!

1 - Sewing Machine Ad

Seam

2

3

4

6 - Theme Paper

5 - Button Card

Place on Fold

I Love Ewe
MATERIALS:
Wool (9" x 23" Green cover, 6" x 7" Gray Tweed Background for #1, 1⅞" x 4⅞" Gold/Green Plaid for #2, 4" x 7" Brown Houndstooth for #3, 1" x 7" Forest Green for #4) • 3" x 4" Muslin • Wool Appliques (**For Sheep**: 2¾" x 4½" Beige, 2" x 3" Dark Brown; **For I Love Ewe**: 1" x 3⅛" Tan; **For Heart Design block**: ⅞" x 1½" Rose, 1" x 1¾" Gold, 1¼" x 2" Green; **For Word Heart block**: ⅞" x 1⅝" Gold, 1¼" x 1⅞" Tan; **For Feed my sheep**: 1⅜" x 2⅜" Coral, 1⅝" x 3" Beige; **For Charm block**: 1⅛" x 1¼" Tan, 1½" x 1¾" Gold) • 2 heart charms • 4 Brown ⅛" brads

• *ColorBox* ink (Light Rose, Light Gray) • Pigma pens (Red, Green) • *DMC* floss (Light Tan, Dark Green, Light Gold, Medium Green, Brown, Yellow, Pink) • Needle • Thread • Steam-A-Seam II
INSTRUCTIONS:
1. Cut out pieces #1-4 using the Wool Placement diagram below. #3 has a pattern on page 30. Apply Steam-A-Seam II to the back of all pieces. Fuse pieces #2-4 in place.
2. Blanket stitch across the bottom and the left long side of #4 with Light Green floss.
3. Cut out all the Wool Appliques. Apply Steam-A-Seam II to all pieces.

1 - Cover Background - 6" x 7" - Gray Tweed

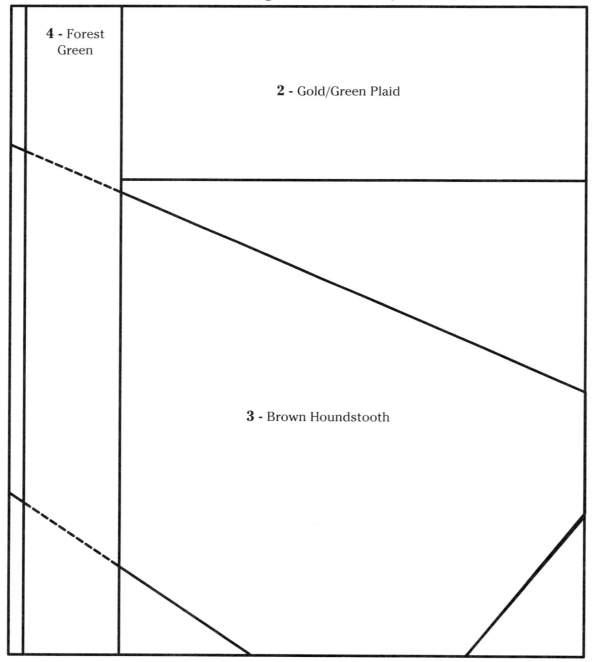

4 - Forest Green

2 - Gold/Green Plaid

3 - Brown Houndstooth

EMBROIDERY:

4. Transfer 4 patterns from page 30 to the Muslin. Backstitch "I Love Ewe" with Dark Green floss and "do you love me..." with Brown floss. Embroider the vine with Dark Green floss. Make flowers with Pink French Knots. Apply Steam-A-Seam II to all 4 pieces. Cut out. To marble the Muslin, lightly apply Gray ink to "do you love me" with a finger or sponge.

5. Write the word "Heart" with a Red Pigma pen. Ink the edges with Rose.

6. Color the Heart design Red and draw Green lines with Pigma pens. Ink the edges with Rose.

APPLIQUE:

7. **I Love Ewe block**: Stack and fuse pieces to the Background. Blanket stitch around the Muslin and Tan wool with Light Tan floss.

8. **Heart Design block**: Stack and fuse pieces together. Blanket stitch around the Muslin, Rose, and Gold wool with 1 strand Light Tan floss. Fuse to Background. Blanket stitch around the Green wool with Light Green floss.

9. **Sheep block**: Trace the reverse side of the patterns for the sheep onto Steam-A-Seam II. Fuse Steam-A-Seam II to wool. Cut out pieces. Draw vine on sheep. Fuse sheep to Background. Fuse nose, ear, and legs in place. Backstitch the vine with Medium Green floss. Embroider Yellow French Knots for the flower centers and Pink French Knots for the petals. Backstitch around the sheep with Light Tan floss. Backstitch the nose and ear with Brown floss. Sew a Running stitch around the edge of each leg with Brown floss.

10. **Heart Words block**: Stack and fuse pieces together. Blanket stitch around the Muslin and Gold wool with 1 strand Light Tan floss. Fuse to Background. Blanket stitch around the Tan wool with Brown floss.

11. **Feed my sheep block**: Stack and fuse pieces together.

Blanket stitch around the Muslin with 1 strand Brown floss. Blanket stitch around the Coral with Light Gold floss. Fuse to Background. Blanket stitch around the wool with Dark Green floss.

12. **Charm block**: Stack and fuse pieces to the Background. Blanket stitch around the Tan wool with Dark Green floss, and around the Gold wool with Light Tan floss.

13. Make the book cover following the General Instructions on page 19.

14. Fuse Background to the book cover. Blanket stitch around Background with Green floss.

15. Sew charms in place. Insert 4 brads in the corners of the "feed my sheep" block.

Actual Size Placement Diagram

I Love Ewe
photo on page 8

**I Love Ewe
Patterns**

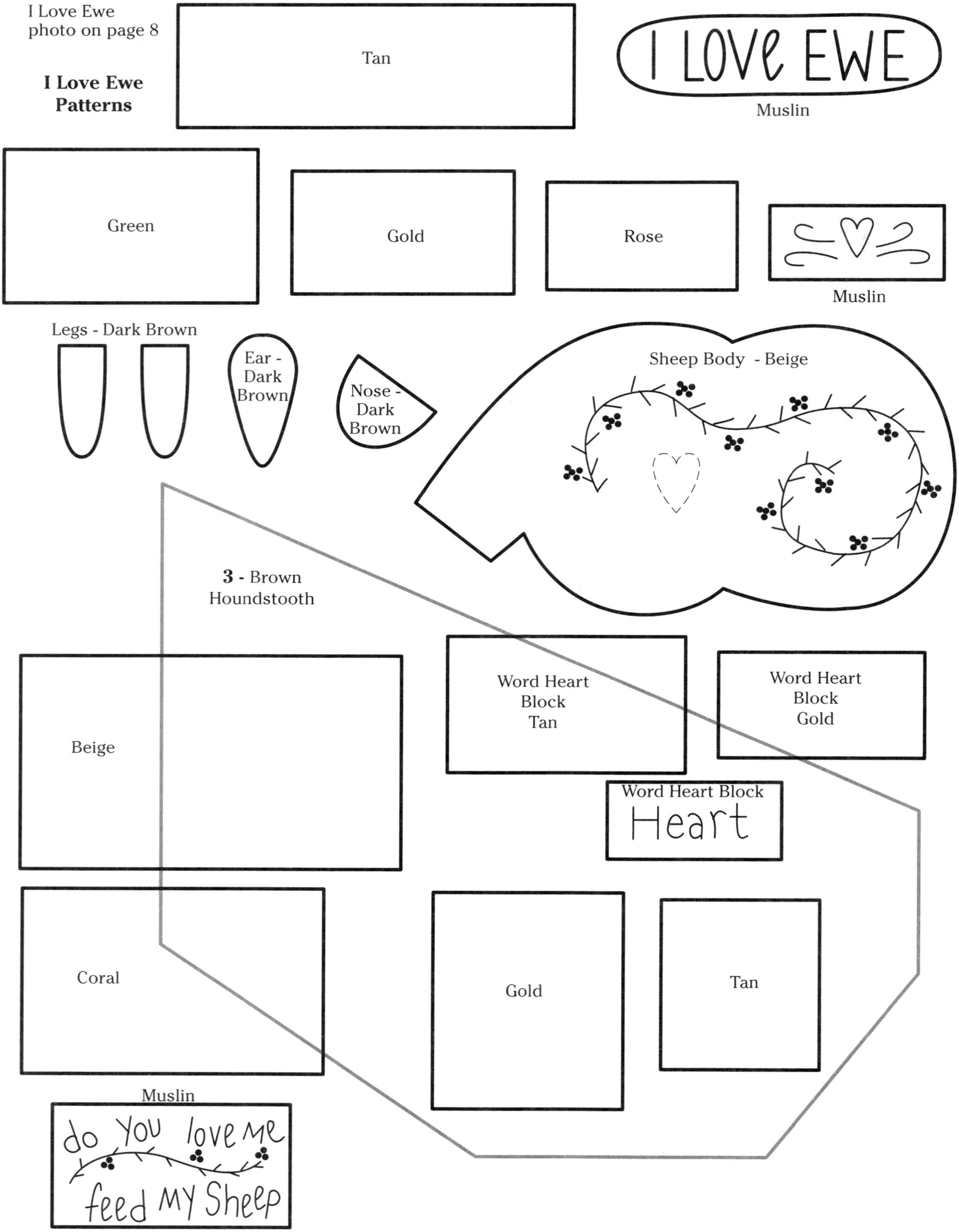

Tan

I LOVE EWE
Muslin

Green

Gold

Rose

Muslin

Legs - Dark Brown

Ear -
Dark
Brown

Nose -
Dark
Brown

Sheep Body - Beige

3 - Brown
Houndstooth

Beige

Word Heart
Block
Tan

Word Heart
Block
Gold

Word Heart Block
Heart

Coral

Gold

Tan

Muslin

do you love me
feed my Sheep

Valentine Purse

MATERIALS:
Wool (4½" x 10½" Pink, 1½" x 3¼" Green, 1" x 2¾" Rose) • ¾" x 2½" Muslin • 1⅜" x 2⅛" Manila cardstock • 1⅜" x 1⅝" collage paper • Black key charm • *DMC* floss (Tan, Rose, Dark Green, Black) • Needle • Thread • Steam-A-Seam II

INSTRUCTIONS:
See General Instructions on page 20. Follow steps 1-8.

Block 1: Trace "St. Valentine" pattern on Muslin. Backstitch with Dark Green floss. Apply Steam-A-Seam II to the back of the Muslin. Cut out oval.

Apply Steam-A-Seam II to all wool pieces. Fuse all pieces in place. Blanket stitch Muslin with Rose floss. Blanket stitch around the Rose wool and Green wool with Tan floss.

Block 2: Copy "Love" definition on Manila cardstock. Cut out. Blanket stitch with Tan floss.

Block 3: Blanket stitch the collage paper in place.

Block 4: Sew key to purse with Black floss.

Continue with Step 9 of the General Instructions on page 20.

Manila Cardstock

Love- (luv) n. 1. a deep and tender feeling of affection or attachment to another, esp. to one of the opposite sex; intense fondness, deep devotion. 2. Courtship. 3. Object of affection. 4. Benevolence; kindness; charity. 5. Passion.

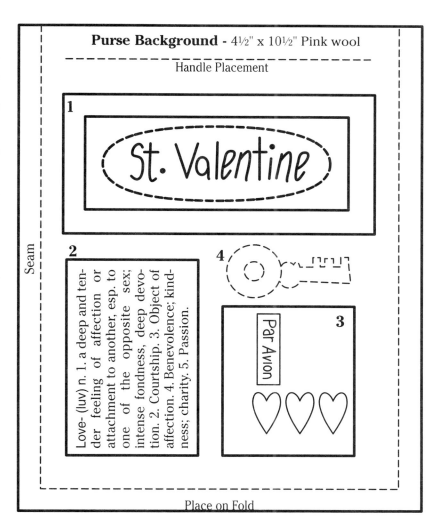

Purse Background - 4½" x 10½" Pink wool

Handle Placement

Seam

Place on Fold

1

St. Valentine

2

Love- (luv) n. 1. a deep and tender feeling of affection or attachment to another, esp. to one of the opposite sex; intense fondness, deep devotion. 2. Courtship. 3. Object of affection. 4. Benevolence; kindness; charity. 5. Passion.

4

3

Par Avion

Green

Rose

Collage paper

St. Valentine

1 - Muslin

Hearts Journal
photo on page 9

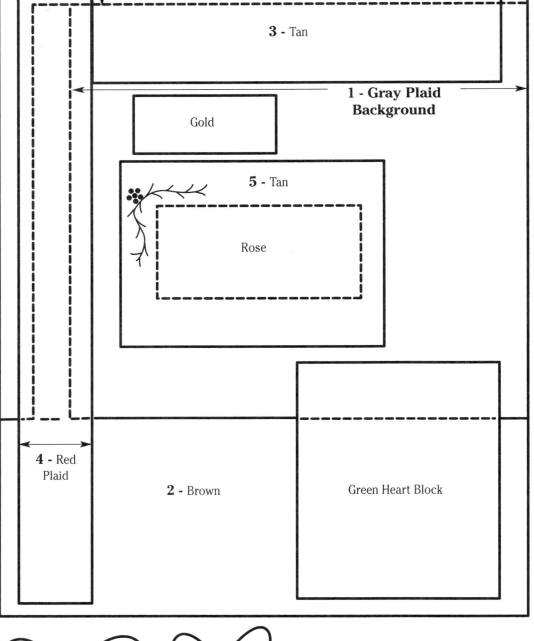

Cover Piece - 4⅞" x 5½" x ³⁄₈" - Red Plaid

3 - Tan

1 - Gray Plaid
Background

Gold

5 - Tan

Rose

4 - Red
Plaid

2 - Brown

Green Heart Block

Red
Plaid

the greatest of these is Love

Rose

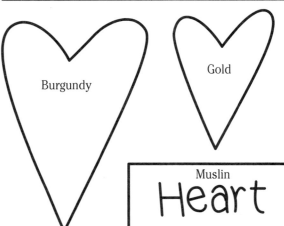

Burgundy

Gold

Muslin
Heart

Pink

Muslin
St. Valentine

Hearts Journal

MATERIALS:

9" x 23" Gold Plaid cotton cover • 2 strips Red Plaid wool ½" x 23" for cover • Wool (4½" x 4⅝" Gray Plaid Background for #1, 2⅛" x 5½" Brown for #2, 1" x 4" Tan for #3, ⅞" x 6⅝" Red Plaid for #4, 2" x 2¾" Tan for #5) • Muslin (⅝" x 2½"; ¾" x 1¾") • Wool Appliques (**For Valentine block**: 1" x 2¾" Pink; **For heart word block**: 1" x 2⅛" Rose; **For Hearts block**: 2⅛" x 2⅝" Green, 2" x 2½" Burgundy, 1¼" x 1¾" Gold; **For vine block**: ⅞" x 2½" Rose; **For Pink Roses block**: ⅝" x 1½" Gold) • Buttons (3 Tan, 3 small Pink rose) • 2 heart charms • ⅛" Red brad • *ColorBox* ink (Rose, Blue) • *DMC* floss (Tan, Light Brown, Green, Red, Pink, Blue) • Needle • Thread • Steam-A-Seam II

INSTRUCTIONS:

1. Make the book cover following the General Instructions on page 19.

2. Cut out Red plaid cover strips and pieces #1-5 using the Wool Placement patterns on page 32. Apply Steam-A-Seam II to the back of all pieces. Fuse pieces #2-5 in place. Fuse Red strips to the cover.

3. Blanket stitch around #3 with Green floss. Blanket stitch around #4 and Backstitch words with Tan floss. Blanket stitch around #5 with Light Brown floss, and around the Red plaid strips with Blue floss.

4. EMBROIDERY: Transfer the embroidery patterns to Muslin. Backstitch "St. Valentine" with Green floss, and "Heart" with Red floss. Apply Steam-A-Seam II. Cut out. Ink edges of "St. Valentine" with Rose. Ink the edges of "Heart" with Rose and Blue.

APPLIQUE:

5. **Valentine block**: Cut Pink wool 1" x 2¾". Apply Steam-A-Seam II. See Placement Diagram. Fuse embroidered words and Pink wool in place. Blanket stitch around the Muslin with Light Brown floss. Blanket stitch around the Pink wool with Tan floss.

6. **Roses block**: Cut Gold wool ½" x 1½". Apply Steam-A-Seam II. Fuse in place. Use a Running stitch around the edge with Light Brown floss.

7. **Heart Words block**: Cut Rose wool 1" x 2⅛". Apply Steam-A-Seam II. Fuse "Heart" embroidery in place. Fuse to #5. Blanket stitch around both with Tan floss. Embroider the flower and vine in the corner. The flowers are French Knots in Pink and Red floss. Backstitch the vines with Green floss.

8. **Vine block**: Cut Rose wool ⅞" x 2½". Apply Steam-A-Seam II. Fuse in place. Embroider the flower and vine just like step 6. Blanket stitch around with Tan floss.

9. **Hearts block**: Cut out Green wool 2⅛" x 2⅝". Trace the Heart patterns in reverse on Steam-A-Seam II. See

page 32. Fuse small heart to Gold wool, and large heart to Burgundy wool. Cut out and fuse in place. Blanket stitch around the Gold heart and Green wool with Green floss. Stitch around the Red heart with Tan floss.

10. Fuse Background to the book cover. Blanket stitch around Background with Tan floss.

11. Sew on buttons and heart charms. Push Red brad through the center of the Gold heart.

Hearts Journal Placement Diagram

Pretty in Pink Journal

MATERIALS:

Wool (9" x 23" Purple cover, 6" x 8" Pink Background for #1, 5¼" x 6½" Light Blue for #2, 2" x 4¾" Light Green #4, 1⅝" x 2¾" Green for #6) • Cotton (2¼" x 4¾" Gold Plaid for #3, 3¼" x 3½" Mauve for #5) • ½" x 3" Muslin • Appliques (**For Castle block #3**: 1¾" x 4¼" Green cotton; **For Sugar and Spice block**: 1½" x 2⅜" Green wool, 1¼" x 2⅛" Mauve wool; **For Ballerina block #4**: 1⅞" x 4⅜" Coral wool; **For photo block #5**: 3¼" x 3½" Mauve; 2⅞" x 2¾" Tan cardstock:; **For Flowers block #6**: 1¼" x 2½" Green calico, 1" x 2¼" Pink wool; **For Princess block**: ⅝" x 3⅜" Coral wool) • *Jolee's By You*: (Paper sandcastle, Ballerina set, Pink party favors, Pink flowers) • *ColorBox* Chestnut Roan ink • *DMC* floss (Brown, Green, Light Blue, Tan, Pink, Lavender, Gold, Light Green, Light Brown) • Tan cardstock • Needle • Thread • Steam-A-Seam II • Fabric glue • Glue stick

INSTRUCTIONS:

1. Cut out pieces #1-6 using the Wool Placement patterns on page 35. Apply Steam-A-Seam II to the back of all pieces. Fuse pieces #2-6 in place.

2. Blanket stitch across the top and 3" down the right side of #2 with Light Blue floss. Blanket stitch #3 with Light Green floss, #4 with Pink floss, #5 with Tan floss, and #6 with Gold floss.

APPLIQUE:

3. **Castle block**: Cut Green cotton 1¾" x 4¼". Apply Steam-A-Seam II. Fuse to #3. Blanket stitch around with Light Brown floss. Adhere paper castle to block.

4. **Sugar and Spice block**: Print "sugar and spice" words on Tan cardstock. Cut out. Cut Green wool 1½" x 2⅜" and Mauve wool 1¼" x 2⅛". Apply Steam-A-Seam II to the back of all pieces. Fuse pieces together. Blanket stitch cardstock with Brown floss, Mauve wool with Light Green floss, and Green wool with Gold floss. Fuse to Castle.

5. **Ballerina block**: Cut Coral wool 1⅞" x 4⅜". Apply Steam-A-Seam II. Fuse in place. Blanket stitch around with Gold floss.

6. **Photo block**: Cut Tan cardstock 2⅞" x 2¾". Apply Steam-A-Seam II. Fuse in place. Blanket stitch with Light Brown floss.

7. **Flowers block**: Cut Green calico 1¼" x 2½" and Pink wool 1" x 2¼". Apply Steam-A-Seam II. Fuse to #6. Blanket stitch around the Pink with Gold floss, and around the Green with Light Brown floss.

8. **Princess block**: Cut Coral wool ⅝" x 3⅜". Copy "Princess" pattern onto Tan cardstock. Apply Steam-A-Seam II. Cut out. Ink the edges. Fuse to Coral wool.

Blanket stitch around with Gold floss. Fuse Coral to the background. Blanket stitch around with Light Green.

9. **Pretty in Pink block**: Transfer the embroidery pattern to the Muslin. Backstitch "Pretty in Pink..." with Pink floss. Apply Steam-A-Seam II. Cut out. Fuse in place. Blanket stitch around with Light Green floss.

10. Make the book cover following the General Instructions on page 19.

11. Fuse Background to the book cover. Blanket stitch around Background with Lavender floss.

12. Photo block: Copy "sweet" definition onto Tan cardstock. Ink the edges. Adhere definition with Fabric glue. Cut out photos Adhere to definition with glue stick.

13. Adhere Jolee's embellishments with Fabric glue. Let dry.

Placement Diagram

Pretty in Pink Patterns Actual Size

1 - Cover Background - 6" x 8" - Pink

2 - Light Blue

3 - Gold Plaid

Light Green

Coral

6 - Green

Green Calico

Pink

4 - Light Green

Coral

5 - Mauve

Photo Block
Tan Cardstock

P
R
I
N
C
E
S
S

Tan
Cardstock

Muslin

Pretty in Pink

Definition
Block
Tan
Cardstock

SWEET, a. [-ER; -EST:] [A.-S *sweet.*]
1. Having a taste like that of sugar. 2.
Pleasing to any sense. 3. Fresh, not
salt. 4. Not changed from a sound or
wholesome state. — *n.* 1. That which
is sweet to the taste. 2. That which is
pleasing to any of the senses or to the
mind. 3. A darling.

Oval
Cardstock

Light Green

Mauve

**Sugar and spice
And everything nice.
That's what little girls
are made of.**

Tan Cardstock

Christina's Journal Pattern Diagram - Actual Size

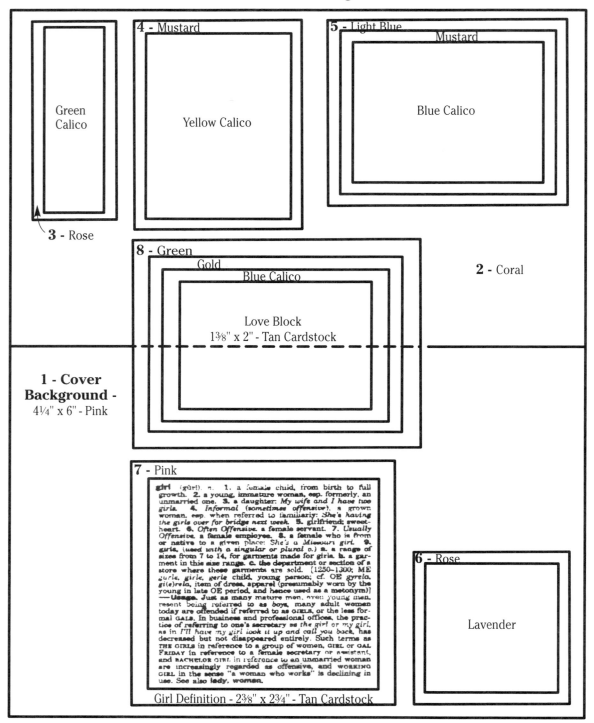

4 - Mustard

5 - Light Blue

Green
Calico

Yellow Calico

Mustard

Blue Calico

3 - Rose

8 - Green

Gold

Blue Calico

2 - Coral

Love Block
1⅜" x 2" - Tan Cardstock

1 - Cover
Background -
4¼" x 6" - Pink

7 - Pink

girl (gûrl). n. 1. a female child, from birth to full growth. 2. a young, immature woman, esp. formerly, an unmarried one. 3. a daughter: *My wife and I have two girls.* 4. *Informal (sometimes offensive).* a grown woman, esp. when referred to familiarly: *She's having the girls over for bridge next week.* 5. girlfriend; sweetheart. 6. *Often Offensive.* a female servant. 7. *Usually Offensive.* a female employee. 8. a female who is from or native to a given place: *She's a Missouri girl.* 9. girls, (used with a singular or plural v.) a. a range of sizes from 7 to 14, for garments made for girls. b. a garment in this size range. c. the department or section of a store where these garments are sold. [1250–1300; ME *gurle, girle, gerle* child, young person; cf. OE *gyrela, gi(e)rela,* item of dress, apparel (presumably worn by the young in late OE period, and hence used as a metonym)] —Usage. Just as many mature men resent young men resent being referred to as boys, many adult women today are offended if referred to as GIRLS, or the less formal GALS. In business and professional offices, the practice of referring to one's secretary as *the girl* or *my girl,* as in *I'll have my girl look it up and call you back,* has decreased but not disappeared entirely. Such terms as THE GIRLS in reference to a group of women, GIRL or GAL FRIDAY in reference to a female secretary or assistant, and BACHELOR GIRL in reference to an unmarried woman are increasingly regarded as offensive, and WORKING GIRL in the sense "a woman who works" is declining in use. See also **lady, woman.**

6 - Rose

Lavender

Girl Definition - 2⅜" x 2¾" - Tan Cardstock

1" x 5¼" - Muslin

follow the truth in Your heart and all your footsteps will be Straight

Christina's Journal

MATERIALS:
Wool (9" x 23" Purple, 4¼" x 6" Pink Background for #1, 3⅝" x 6" Coral for #2, ⅞" x 2¼" Rose for #3, 1¾" x 2¼" Mustard #4, 2" x 2½" Light Blue for #5, 1⅝" square Rose for #6, 2¼" x 3" Green for #8) • 2⅝" x 2⅝" Pink cotton for #7 • 1" x 5¼" Muslin • Appliques (**Learn Block:** 1½" x 2" Yellow calico; **Create Block:** 1¾" x 2¼" Mustard wool, 1½" x 2" Blue calico; **Love Block:** 2" x 2⅝" Gold wool, 1⅝" x 2⅜" Blue calico; **For Feet Block:** 1⅜" square Lavender wool; **For Girl Block:** ⅝" x 2" Green calico) • *Jolee's By You*: (Yellow paper notebook with pencils, School English book, Coloring set, Pink footprints paper, Heart card with envelope, Metal stick-on letters, Christening gown, Pink bear) • *ColorBox* Chestnut Roan ink • *DMC* floss (Brown, Tan, Gold, Light Yellow, Pink, Dark Pink, Lavender) • Tan cardstock • Needle • Thread • Steam-A-Seam II • Fabric glue • Glue stick

Fuse to #6. Blanket stitch around with Pink floss.
8. Make the book cover following the General Instructions on page 19.
9. Fuse Background to the book cover. Blanket stitch around Background with Lavender floss.
10. Photo block: Copy "girl" definition onto 2⅜" x 2⅜" Tan cardstock. Ink the edges. Adhere definition with Fabric glue. Cut out photos Adhere to definition with glue stick.
11. Print "learn" and "create" on a paper. Cut out. Adhere in place. Adhere embellishments with fabric glue. Let dry.

INSTRUCTIONS:
1. Cut out pieces #1-8 using the Wool Placement patterns on page 36. Apply Steam-A-Seam II to the back of all pieces. Fuse pieces #2-8 in place.
2. Blanket stitch around #3 with Tan floss. Stitch #5, #6, and #8 with Light Yellow floss. Stitch #4 with Gold floss and #7 with Dark Pink floss.
3. EMBROIDERY: Transfer the embroidery pattern to the Muslin. Backstitch "follow the truth..." with Brown floss. Apply Steam-A-Seam II. Cut out. Ink the edges with Chestnut Roan. Fuse in place. Blanket stitch around with Tan floss.
APPLIQUE:
4. **Girl block:** Cut Green calico ⅝" x 2". Apply Steam-A-Seam II. Fuse to #3. Blanket stitch around with Tan floss.
5. **Learn block:** Cut Yellow calico 1½" x 2". Apply Steam-A-Seam II. Fuse in place. Blanket stitch around with Pink floss.
6. **Create block:** Cut Mustard wool 1¾" x 2¼" and Blue calico 1½" x 2". Apply Steam-A-Seam II to both pieces. Fuse in place. Blanket stitch the Mustard with Pink floss. Blanket stitch the calico with Light Yellow floss.
7. **Feet block:** Cut a 1⅜" square of Lavender wool. Apply Steam-A-Seam II.

Placement Diagram

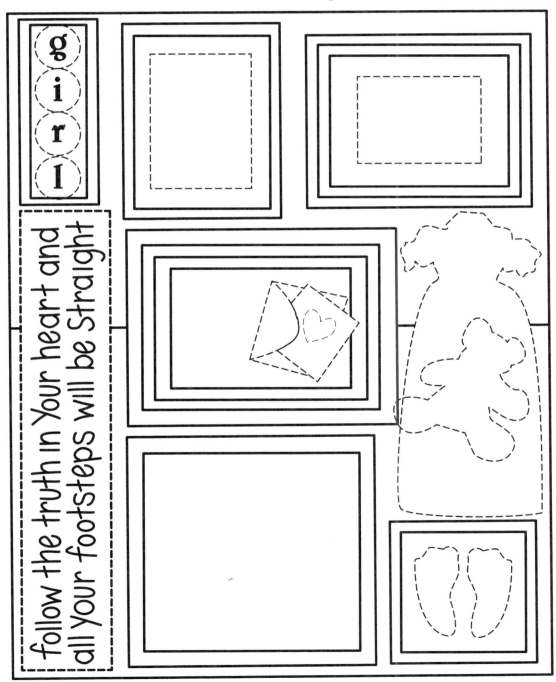

Sew Journal
photo on page 7

Journal
General
Instructions
on page 19

Sew Journal
MATERIALS:
Wool (9" x 23" Red/Navy Plaid cover, 5½" x 7¾" Dark Brown Background for #1, 1½" x 4½" Navy/Tan Houndstooth for #2, 1" x 7¾" Gold for #3, 1¼" square Forest Green for #4, 1" x 1½" Navy/Tan Houndstooth for #5, 2" x 2½" Brown Tweed for #6, 1⅛" x 2¾" Forest Green for #7, 2¾" x 3¼" Brown/White Houndstooth for #8) • 4" square Muslin • Wool Appliques (**For #2:** 1½" square Black, 1½" square Navy/Tan Houndstooth, 1½" square Brown Plaid, 1¾" square Tan; **For #4:** ⅞"

square Tan; **For #5:** Tan ¾" x 1¼"; **For #8:** 1⅜" x 1½" Gold, 1⅞" square Plum, 2" x 2⅜" Forest Green) • 1" x 1½" wool Fabric Swatches for #6 (Red, Forest Green, Rust, Gray, Gold, Pink, Sage) • 7⅛" tape measure • *Jolee's By You* small scissors charm • Small wood hand charm • Buttons (1 Black ¾", 5 Forest Green ³⁄₁₆") • 3 Black ⅛" brads • Manila cardstock scrap • *ColorBox* Chestnut Roan ink • *DMC* floss (Tan, Green, Black, Brown, Light Brown, Forest Green, Light Blue, Gray, Dark Blue, Rose, Rust, Gold, Red, Dark Brown, Mustard) • Needle • Thread • Steam-A-Seam II • E6000

1 - Dark Brown Background - 5½" x 7¾"

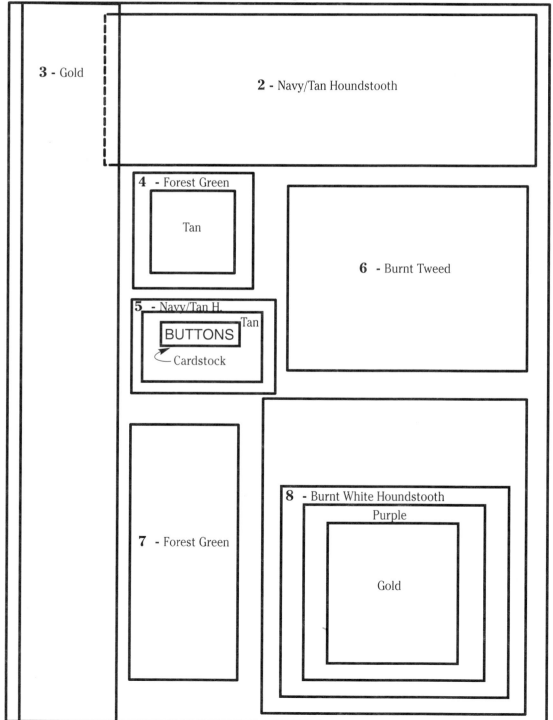

INSTRUCTIONS:
1. Cut out pieces #1-8 using the Wool Pattern placement diagram on this page. Apply Steam-A-Seam II to the back of all pieces. Fuse pieces #2-8 in place.
2. Blanket stitch around #2, #5, #6, and #8 with Tan floss. Blanket stitch around #3, #4, and #7 with Green floss.

Manila Cardstock Pattern for Floss Sampler

Floss Guide Line Pattern

—
Green
Forest Green
Light Blue
Gray
Dark Blue
Rose
Rust
Gold
Red
Dark Brown
Light Brown
Mustard
Tan
—

3. Draw the shapes and transfer letters "S", "e", "w", and "the work of my hands" to Muslin. Backstitch the "S" with Brown floss, the "e" and "w" with Black floss. The dots are French Knots. • Backstitch "the work of my hands" with Green floss.

4. Apply Steam-A-Seam II to the back of the embroidery. Cut out the shapes. Ink the edges of the "S", "e", and "w".

APPLIQUE:

5. Fuse "the work of my hands" to #8. Blanket stitch with Black floss.

6. **Block #2**: Trace the patterns on Steam-A-Seam II. Fuse to fabric. Cut out. Fuse all pieces to #2. Backstitch around the Black circle, Brown tag, and Navy/Tan Houndstooth circle with Tan floss. Backstitch around the Tan circle with Green floss. Pierce brads through tags and Background.

7. **Block #4**: Cut a Tan ⅞" square. Fuse Steam-A-Seam II to the back. Fuse to #4. Blanket stitch around with Green floss.

8. **Block #5**: Cut a Tan ¾" x 1¼". Fuse Steam-A-Seam II to the back. Fuse to #5. Blanket stitch around with Tan floss.

9. **Block #6**: Trace patterns for 1" x 1½" fabric swatches onto Steam-A-Seam II. Press to fabric. Arrange in a fan on Block 6. Fuse in place. Blanket stitch around swatches with Green floss.

10. **Block #7**: Cut out ¾" x 2⅜"cardstock pattern for floss sam-ples. Draw guide lines with a pencil. Wrap floss following the pattern. Set aside.

11. **Block #8**: Cut out Gold 1¼" x 1½", Plum 1⅞" square, and Forest Green 2" x 2⅜". Fuse Steam-A-Seam II to the back of all pieces. Stack and fuse all pieces in place. Blanket stitch around the Gold with Green floss, around the Plum with Tan floss, and around the Forest Green with Green floss.

12. Make the book cover following the General Instructions on page 19.

13. Fuse Background to the book cover. Blanket stitch around Background with Tan floss.

14. Sew charms and buttons in place.

15. Computer print the word "buttons" on cardstock with Green ink. Cut out and glue in place with E6000. Adhere floss sample to #7 and tape measure to #3 with E6000. Let dry.

Placement Diagram

1 - Dark Blue Background - 5⅞" x 7¾" - Actual Size

3 - Blue Houndstooth

Train Block
Gold

2 - Navy
Houndstooth

5 - Light Blue

Blue Houndstooth

Hands Block

Periwinkle

4 - Navy Pillow
Ticking

6 - Navy

boy (boi), *n.* **1.** a male child, from birth to full growth, esp. one less than 18 years of age. **2.** a young man who lacks maturity, judgment, etc. **3.** *Informal.* a grown man, esp. when referred to familiarly: *He liked to play poker with the boys.* **4.** a son: *Sam's oldest boy is helping him in the business.* **5.** a male who is from or native to a given place. **6. boys,** (used with a singular or plural v.) **a.** a range of sizes from 8 to 20 in garments made for boys. **b.** a garment in this size range. **c.** the department or section of a store where these garments are sold. **7. boys,** military personnel, esp. combat soldiers: *Support the boys overseas.* **8.** *Disparaging and Offensive.* a man considered by the speaker to be inferior in race, nationality, or occupational status. **9.** a young male servant; page. **10.** *Offensive.* (in India, China, Japan, etc.) a native male servant, working as a butler, waiter, houseboy, etc. **11.** *Naut.* an apprentice seaman or fisherman. —*interj.* **12.** an exclamation of wonder, approval, etc., or of displeasure or contempt. [1250–1300; ME boy(e), perh. after OE *Bóia* man's name; c. Fris boi young man; akin to OE *bófa,* ON *bófi,* OHG *Buobo* man's name (G *Bube* knave, (dial.) boy, lad)]

Tan Cardstock Definition - 2¼" x 2¾"

7 - Green

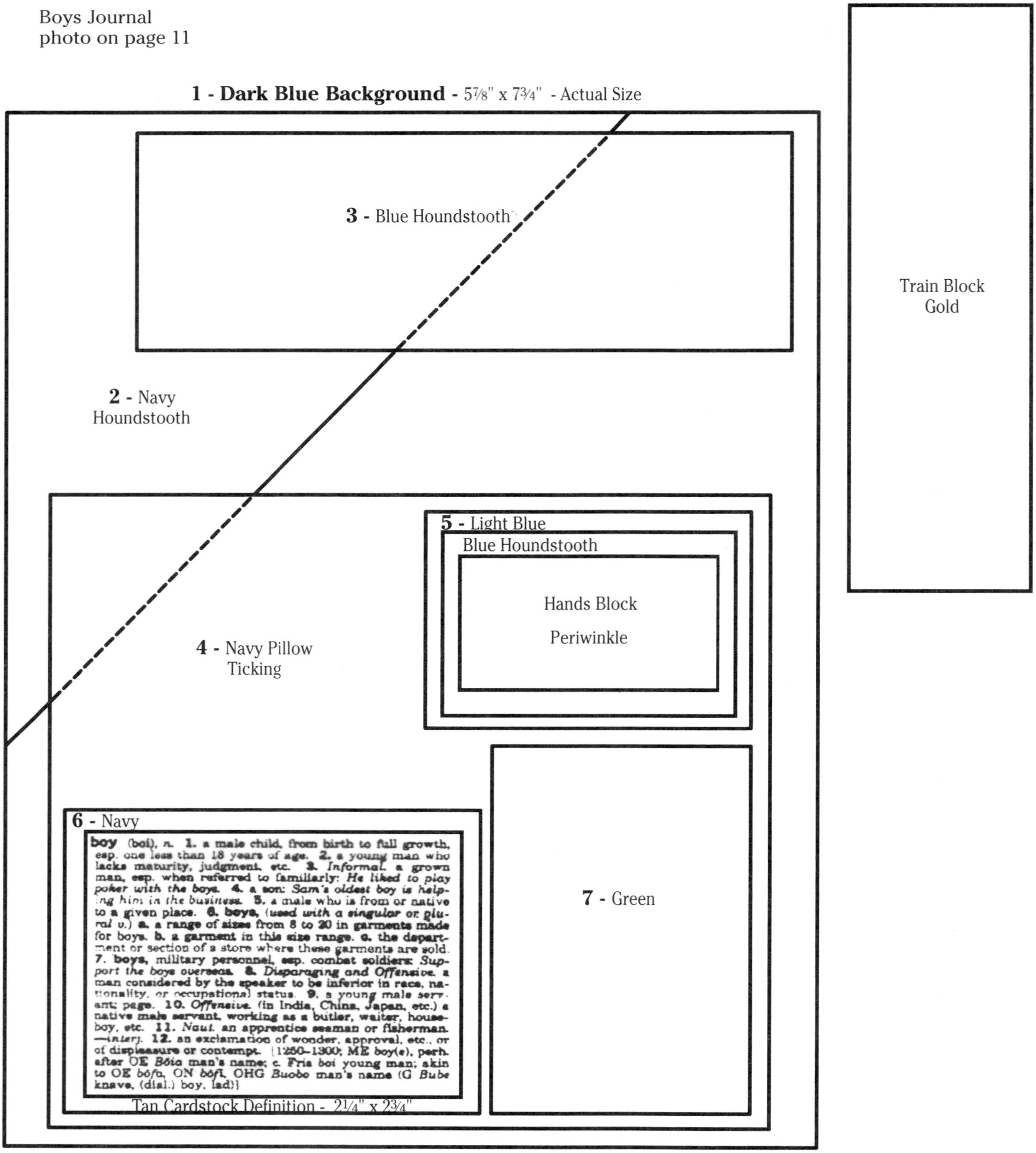

Muslin - ⅞" x 5¼"

as you grow the fingerprints of who you are will remain the same

Boy's Journal

MATERIALS:

Wool (9" x 23" Light Blue cover, 5¾" x 7¾" Dark Blue Background for #1, 5" square Navy Houndstooth for #2, 1½" x 4¾" Blue Houndstooth for #3, 1½" x 2½" Light Blue for #5, 2¼" x 3" Navy for #6, 1⅞" x 2¾" Green for #7, 1⅞" x 1⅞" Light Blue for #8) • 4¾" x 5⅛" Navy pillow ticking for #4 • 1" x 5" Muslin • Wool Appliques (**For #3:** 1¼" x 4¼" Gold; **For #5:** 1¼" x 2" Blue Houndstooth, 1" x 1¾" Periwinkle; **For #8:** 1⅝" square Blue Houndstooth) • *Jolee's By You:* (Wood train set, Blue bear, Hand prints, Baseball set, Metal stick-on letters) • *ColorBox* Chestnut Roan ink • *DMC* floss (Brown, Gray, Tan, Light Blue) • Tan cardstock • Needle • Thread • Steam-A-Seam II • Fabric glue • Glue stick

INSTRUCTIONS:

1. Cut out pieces #1-8 using the Wool Placement patterns. Apply Steam-A-Seam II to the back of all pieces. Fuse pieces #2-8 in place.

2. Blanket stitch around #3, #5 and #6 with Tan floss. Stitch #4, #7 and #8 with Gray floss.

3. EMBROIDERY: Transfer the embroidery pattern to the Muslin. Backstitch "As you grow..." with Brown floss. Apply Steam-A-Seam II. Cut out. Ink the edges with Chestnut Roan. Fuse in place. Blanket stitch around with Tan floss.

APPLIQUE:

4. **Train block**: Cut Gold wool 1¼" x 4¼". Apply Steam-A-Seam II. Fuse to #3. Blanket stitch around with Brown floss.

5. **Bear block**: Cut a 1⅝" square of Blue Houndstooth. Apply Steam-A-Seam II. Fuse in place. Blanket stitch around the Houndstooth with Tan floss.

6. **Hands block**: Cut a 1¼" x 2" Blue Houndstooth. Cut a 1" x 1¾" Periwinkle Blue. Apply Steam-A-Seam II to both pieces. Fuse in place. Blanket stitch the Periwinkle with Tan floss. Blanket stitch the Houndstooth with Brown floss.

7. Make the book cover following the General Instructions on page 19.

8. Fuse Background to the book cover. Blanket stitch around Background with Light Blue floss.

9. **Boy block**: Copy "boy" definition onto Tan cardstock. Ink the edges. Adhere definition with Fabric glue. Cut out photos. Adhere to definition with glue stick.

10. Adhere Jolee's embellishments with Fabric glue. Let dry.

Placement Diagram

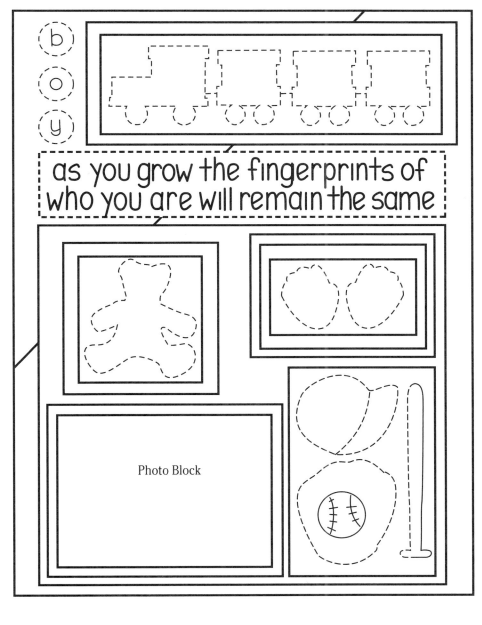

8 - Light Blue

Bear Block
Blue

Bear Block
Blue Houndstooth

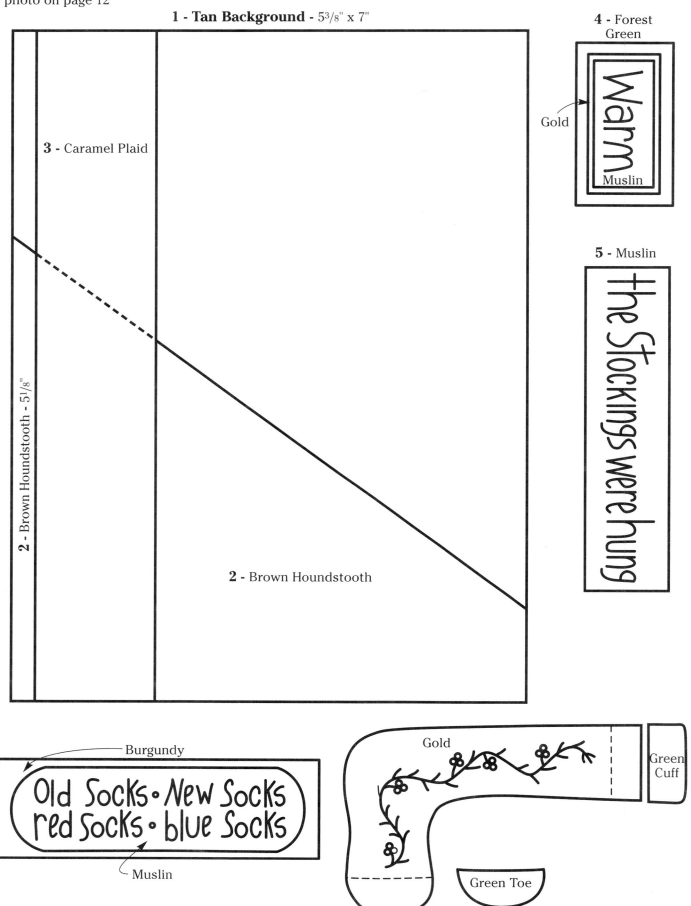

1 - Tan Background - 5³/₈" x 7"

3 - Caramel Plaid

2 - Brown Houndstooth - 5¹/₈"

2 - Brown Houndstooth

4 - Forest Green

Gold

Warm

Muslin

5 - Muslin

the Stockings were hung

Burgundy

Old Socks • New Socks
red Socks • blue Socks

Muslin

Gold

Green Cuff

Green Toe

Socks Journal

MATERIALS:
Wool (9" x 23" Green Plaid cover, 5⅜" x 7" Tan for Background #1, 5" x 5⅜" Brown Houndstooth for #2, 1¼" x 7" Caramel Plaid for #3, 1" x 1¾" Forest Green for #4, ⅞" x 3½" White for #5) • 4" square Muslin • Wool appliques (**For Warm Block:** ¾" x 1½" Gold; **For Old Socks:** 1" x 3⅜" Burgundy; **For star sock:** 3" x 7" Light Tan, 1" square Black tweed for cuff; **For stripe sock:** 2" square Brown for foot, 1" x 3" White; **For Vine sock:** 2½" x 3¼" Gold, 1" square Green for cuff and toe) • *DMC* floss (Red, Green, Dark Green, Dark Brown, Tan, Black, Brown, White) • ⅛" Brads (Red, Brown) • Buttons (1 Green, 2 Red heart, 3 metal stars) • Needle • Thread • Steam-A-Seam II • E6000

INSTRUCTIONS:
1. Cut out pieces #1-5 using the patterns on page 42. Apply Steam-A-Seam II to the back of all pieces. Fuse pieces #2-5 in place.
2. Blanket stitch the diagonal of #2 and all around #4 and #5 with Tan floss. Blanket stitch the long sides of #3 with Dark Brown floss.
3. WORDS EMBROIDERY: Transfer the embroidery patterns to the Muslin and #5. Backstitch "the stockings were hung" on #5 with Red floss. Backstitch "Warm" with Red floss. Backstitch "Old socks" with Dark Green floss. Make French knots with Red floss. Apply Steam-A-Seam II to Muslin pieces. Cut out.

APPLIQUE:
4. Embroider the vine below the "the stockings were hung" with Red French Knots. Backstitch the vine with Green floss.
5. **Warm block:** Cut a ¾" x 1½" Gold wool rectangle and fuse embroidery in place. Fuse to #4 on Background. Blanket stitch around Muslin with Tan floss, around Gold wool with Green floss.
6. **Old socks block:** Fuse embroidery to #5. Use a Running stitch around edge of Muslin with a single strand of Dark Green floss.
7. **Wool stockings:** Trace the reverse of the patterns onto Steam-A-Seam II. Cut out and press to wool. Cut out and press in place following the placement diagram below.
8. **Stars sock:** Satin stitch stars with 3 strands Brown floss. Blanket stitch around with Black floss. Insert a small Red brad through fabric at top of the stocking.
9. **Striped sock:** Whipstitch around stocking with White floss. Blanket stitch Brown toe with Brown floss. For each stripe, use 6 strands Red floss and sew across twice.
10. **Vine sock:** Draw vine and Backstitch with 4 strands of Green floss. Make French Knots with Red floss for the berries. Blanket stitch with Brown floss. Insert a small Brown brad through the fabric at the top of the stocking.
11. Sew the buttons in place.
12. Make book cover following General Instructions on page 19.
13. Fuse to book cover. Blanket stitch all around the Background with Tan floss.

Black Tweed Cuff

Light Tan Stocking

White Stocking

Red Floss Stripes

Brown

Placement Diagram

the Stockings were hung

Warm

Old Socks • New Socks
red Socks • blue Socks

Multiply Journal
photo on page 13

Multiply Journal Pattern Diagram - Actual Size

1 - Gold

2 - Dark Red

What You give from Your heart
Will be Multiplied back to You.

3 - Muslin

4 - Muslin

1	2	3	4	5	6	7	8	9	10	11	12
2	4	6	8	10	12	14	16	18	20	22	24
3	6	9	12	15	18	21	24	27	30	33	36
4	8	12	16	20	24	28	32	36	40	44	48
5	10	15	20	25	30	35	40	45	50	55	60
6	12	18	24	30	36	42	48	54	60	66	72
7	14	21	28	35	42	49	56	63	70	77	84
8	16	24	32	40	48	56	64	72	80	88	96
9	18	27	36	45	54	63	72	81	90	99	108
10	20	30	40	50	60	70	80	90	100	110	120
11	22	33	44	55	66	77	88	99	110	121	132
12	24	36	48	60	72	84	96	108	120	132	144

Multiply Journal

MATERIALS:
Wool (9" x 23" Red/Black Check cover, 1½" x 5½" Dark Red for #2, 1¾" x 6¼" Gold for #1) • Muslin (1" x 5"; 9" x 9") • 1 tea bag • *DMC* floss (Gray, Red, Tan) • Needle • Thread

INSTRUCTIONS:
1. Brew 1 cup of tea. Remove tea bag. Immerse large muslin until it is the desired color. Let dry. Press flat.
2. Trace the grid and numbers onto the tea dyed muslin. Backstitch the grid lines with Gray floss. Backstitch the numbers with Red floss. Press. Trim to size of pattern.
3. Cut out remaining pieces.
4. Backstitch words on small Muslin with Gray floss.
5. Apply Steam-A-Seam II to all pieces.
6. Fuse Muslin words to Red wool.
7. Blanket stitch around Muslin words with Gray floss.
8. Fuse Red wool to the Gold. Blanket stitch around the Red wool with Tan floss.
9. Make the book cover following the General Instructions on page 19.
10. Fuse the grid and Gold to the book cover.
11. Blanket stitch around the edge with Gray floss.

Actual Size Patterns

Muslin

Games People Play

Muslin

tic-tac-toe

Muslin

go-fish

Tic-Tac-Toe
Pink Wool

Go-Fish
Pink Wool

Muslin

B	I	n	g	O
12	25	40	59	62
17	16	36	47	75
1	21	free	51	64
3	20	42	60	71
14	18	45	52	73

Scrabble Block - Light Green Wool

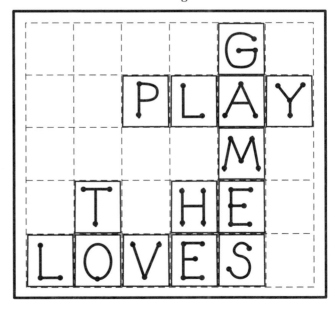

Scrabble
Block - Word
Tiles Pattern
Cut 14

Patterns continued on page 46

Games Journal Placement Diagram

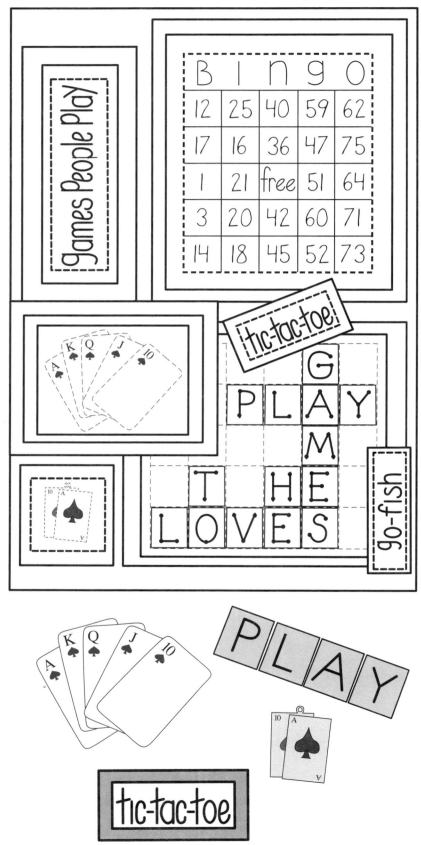

Games People Play Journal

MATERIALS:
Wool (9" x 23" Forest Green cover, 5⅜" x 8" Green Background for #1, 1½" x 3½" Brown/Tan Tweed for #2, 3⅜" x 3¾" Red for #3, 3⅜" x 3¾" Black/Tan plaid for #4, 1¼" x 1⅜" Red for #5) • ⅛ yard Muslin • Royal Flush mini cards • Cards charm • *DMC* floss (Red, Gray, Medium Brown, Medium Green, Light Green, Tan, Black, Green) • Needle • Thread • Steam-A-Seam II • E6000

INSTRUCTIONS:
1. Cut out pieces #1-5 using the patterns on page 47. Apply Steam-A-Seam II to the back of all pieces. Fuse pieces 2-5 in place.
2. Blanket stitch around #2, #4 and #5 with Tan floss. Stitch #3 with Medium Brown floss.

EMBROIDERY:
3. Transfer the embroidery patterns to the Muslin. Backstitch "Games People Play" with Green floss, Bingo numbers and words in Red floss, Bingo grid and Free space in Gray floss. Backstitch Tic-Tac-Toe and Go Fish in Red floss. Backstitch scrabble letters in Black floss with French Knot accents. Apply Steam-A-Seam II to all pieces. Cut out.

APPLIQUE:
4. **Games People Play block**: Cut 1" x 3" Dark Gray wool and fuse embroidery in place. Fuse to #2 on Background. Blanket stitch around ¾" x 2⅝" Muslin with Tan floss, around Gray wool with Brown floss.
5. **Bingo block**: Cut 3" x 3½" Gold wool and fuse embroidery in place. Fuse to #3 on Background. Blanket stitch around 2½" x 3" Muslin with Gray floss, around Gold wool with Medium Green floss.
6. **Scrabble block**: Cut 2⅞" x 3¼" Light Green wool and fuse embroidery in place. Add scrabble grid lines with Black floss. Fuse scrabble letters to Light Green. Fuse to #4 on Background. Blanket stitch around Light Green wool with Medium Green floss.
7. **Card Charm block**: Cut a 1" square of Muslin. Fuse to #5 on background. Blanket stitch edge with Light Green floss. Sew cards charm in place.
8. **Royal Flush block**: Cut 2⅛" x 2⅝" of Brown wool. Cut 1¾" x 2⅜" Gold wool. Cut 1½" x 2" Black/Green Check. Apply Steam-A-Seam II to the back of all pieces. Layer pieces onto background, covering the edge of the Scrabble square. Fuse in place. Blanket stitch the Brown and Check wools with Medium Brown floss. Blanket stitch the Gold wool with Green floss. Glue Royal Flush cards in place.
9. **Tic-Tac-Toe block**: Cut ¾" x 1½" Pink wool. Apply Steam-A-Seam II to the back. Fuse embroidery in place. Blanket stitch Muslin with Tan floss. Fuse to background, following Placement Diagram. Blanket stitch around Pink wool with Medium Green floss.
10. **Go Fish block**: Cut 9/16" x 1¾" Pink wool. Apply Steam-A-Seam II to the back. Fuse embroidery in place. Blanket stitch Muslin with Tan floss. Fuse to background, following Placement Diagram. Blanket stitch around Pink wool with Medium Green floss.
11. Make the book cover following the General Instructions on page 19.
12. Fuse Background to book cover. Blanket stitch around with Tan floss.

Games Journal Pattern Diagram - Actual Size

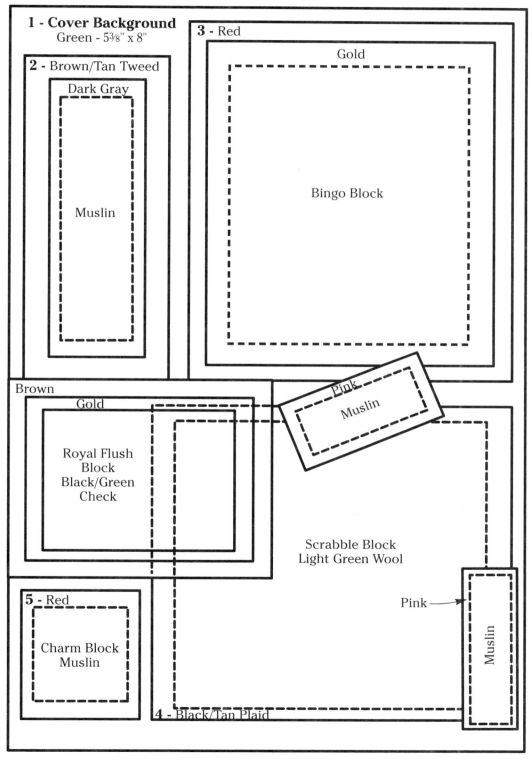

1 - Cover Background
Green - 5⅜" x 8"

2 - Brown/Tan Tweed

Dark Gray

Muslin

3 - Red

Gold

Bingo Block

Brown

Gold

Royal Flush
Block
Black/Green
Check

Pink

Muslin

Scrabble Block
Light Green Wool

Pink

Muslin

5 - Red

Charm Block
Muslin

4 - Black/Tan Plaid

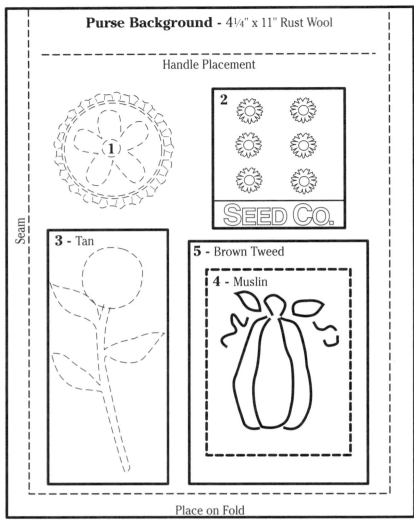

Purse Background - 4¼" x 11" Rust Wool

Handle Placement

Seam

1

2

SEED CO.

3 - Tan

5 - Brown Tweed

4 - Muslin

Place on Fold

Muslin Seed Packet Patterns

Watermelon

Seeds

radish

Seeds

Carrot

Seeds

Seeds Purse

MATERIALS:
Wool (4¼" x 11" Rust, 2" x 2½" Brown Tweed, 1¼" x 2⅞" Tan) • 1⅜" x 1⅝" "seed packet" theme paper • *Design Originals* (Silver bottle cap, #0500 TeaDye Keys paper) • 1½" x 2" Muslin • *Jolee's By You* assorted embellishments • Markers (Black, Orange, Green) • *DMC* floss (Tan, Brown, Dark Brown) • Needle • Thread • 1" circle punch • Small nail • Hammer • Rubber mallet • E6000

INSTRUCTIONS:
See General Instructions on page 20. Follow steps 1-8.

Block 1: Flatten a bottle cap. Punch 2 holes in the center of each cap. Sew to purse. • Punch a circle of TeaDye paper and glue it to the bottle cap. • Glue flower in place.

Block 2: Blanket stitch the "seed packet" paper in place with Brown floss.

Block 3: Blanket stitch the Tan wool in place with Dark Brown floss. • Adhere the sunflower.

Block 4: Draw a pumpkin on the muslin. Backstitch pumpkin lines with Brown floss, leaves and stems with Green floss. Color the pumpkin with markers. • Blanket stitch Muslin to the Tweed with Dark Brown floss. • Blanket stitch Tweed to purse with Tan floss.

Continue with Step 9 of the General Instructions on page 20.

Tip: The frame used in this project is an antique. You may want to size your project to fit a standard frame.

Onion

Seeds

grape

Seeds

Pear

Seeds

Framed Seed Art

MATERIALS:

½ yard Red White Check fabric • ¼ yard Green print border fabric • ⅛ yard Muslin • ⅛ yard Houndstooth suiting • Wool (2" x 2½" Rust, 3" x 3" Dark Brown, 1¼" x 3" Pink, 4" x 4" Black Tweed, ⅛ yard Gold, 2" x 7¼" Green) • 13½" x 17" wood frame • 9 shipping tags 2⅜" x 4" • *Jolee's By You* Mini fruits and vegetables • Craft pitchfork • Chinese coin closure • Nostalgiques (Letter stickers, 2 metal buttons) • 9 Brass brads • Tan cardstock • *DMC* floss (Green, Red, Brown, Tan) • *ColorBox* Chestnut Roan ink • Black pigma pen • Needle • Thread • Warm & Natural cotton batting • E6000

INSTRUCTIONS:

1. Cut a Red Check fabric center block and batting 11½" x 15½". • Pin the batting behind the center block.

2. Cut 2 side border strips 1½" x 17½". • Cut 2 top and bottom border strips 1½" x 13½". • Adhere Steam-A-Seam II to the back. Position strips on center block. See placement diagram on page 53. Press in place. • Blanket stitch the inside border with Green floss, going through the batting.

3. **Seed Packet blocks**: Press Steam-A-Seam II to the shipping tags below the fold line and on the back. See Diagram 1 on page 53. • Cover each tag with Houndstooth suiting. Press to adhere. • Fold the top edge of tag down over fabric. Glue in place with E6000. Ink the tag flap. Punch a hole at the top of the tag and insert a Brass brad.

4. Draw 9 1⅞" x 2⅝"rectangles onto Muslin using patterns on pages 48 - 50. Trace the words onto the Muslin. Backstitch words with Green floss. Underline with a Red Backstitch. • Cut out each rectangle. Apply Steam-A-Seam II. • Ink the edges of the Muslin rectangles.

5. Cut nine 2⅛" x 2¹³⁄₁₆". Gold rectangles for seed packet fronts. See Pattern on page 52. • Fuse Muslin to Gold rectangles. Blanket stitch around the Gold and Muslin with Green floss. • Apply Steam-A-Seam II to Gold wool. Press to seed packet.

6. Press the seed packets in place on the Red background. Blanket stitch around the edge with Red floss.

7. **Title block**: Cut Muslin 1½" x 6¾". Cut Green wool 2⅛" x 7¼". Apply Steam-A-Seam II to both pieces. Fuse Muslin to Green wool. Blanket stitch around the Muslin with Red floss. Fuse to Red background. Blanket stitch around the Green wool with Brown floss. • From Black Tweed, cut one for J Block and pattern C Block. From Muslin, cut 1 from patterns on page 50. Apply Steam-A-Seam II to all pieces. Press Muslin onto Tweed following the placement diagram. Blanket stitch the Muslin with Green floss. Fuse the Black Tweed to the title Muslin. Blanket stitch with Tan floss. • Cut Muslin ⅞" x 2⅝". Trace word "Seed" with Black pigma pen. See pattern on page 50. • Apply Steam-A-Seam II to the Pink wool and Muslin. Fuse Muslin to Pink wool. Blanket stitch Muslin with Green floss. Fuse in place. Blanket stitch edge of Pink wool with Tan floss. • Cut 2 Brown wool circles on page 52. Cut 2 Muslin circles on page 52. Blanket stitch Muslin to Brown wool with Brown floss. Apply Steam-A-Seam II and fuse to background. Blanket stitch around the edge with Tan floss.

8. **You will reap block**: Draw a 1½" x 2" rectangle on Muslin. Trace the words "You will reap what you sow" from page 52. Backstitch with Green floss. Cut out the rectangle. Apply Steam-A-Seam II to all pieces. Fuse stitched Muslin to the Rust wool. Blanket stitch around with Brown floss. • Fuse the Rust wool to the background. Blanket stitch with Green floss.

9. **Seed Definition block**: Copy the "seed definition" from page 52 onto Tan cardstock. • Cut out and ink the edges. • Cut Houndstooth suiting 2¹⁄₂" x 3⅝". Apply Steam-A-Seam II to the definition and Houndstooth. Fuse the definition to the Houndstooth and fuse the rectangle to the background. Blanket stitch the edge with Red floss.

10. **While the earth remains block**: Cut Gold 2⅜" x 3⅜". • Draw a 1⅞" x 3⅛" rectangle on Muslin. Trace the words "While the earth remains" from page 53. Backstitch with Red floss. Cut out the rectangle. Apply Steam-A-Seam II to all pieces. Fuse stitched Muslin to the Gold wool. Blanket stitch around the Muslin with Brown floss. • Fuse the Gold wool to the background. Blanket stitch with Green floss.

11. Sew pitchfork in place. Adhere Chinese coins, buttons, stickers, and paper fruits and vegetables with E6000. Let dry completely.

12. Frame the project.

Pear

Seed Packet Patterns
Muslin

Seeds

apple

Seeds

Block J
Black Tweed

Block J
Muslin

Block J

pepper

Seeds

Cucumber

Seeds

Block C - Black Tweed

Muslin

Block C

C

Muslin

Seed Block - Pink

SEED

Title Block - Green Wool

Muslin

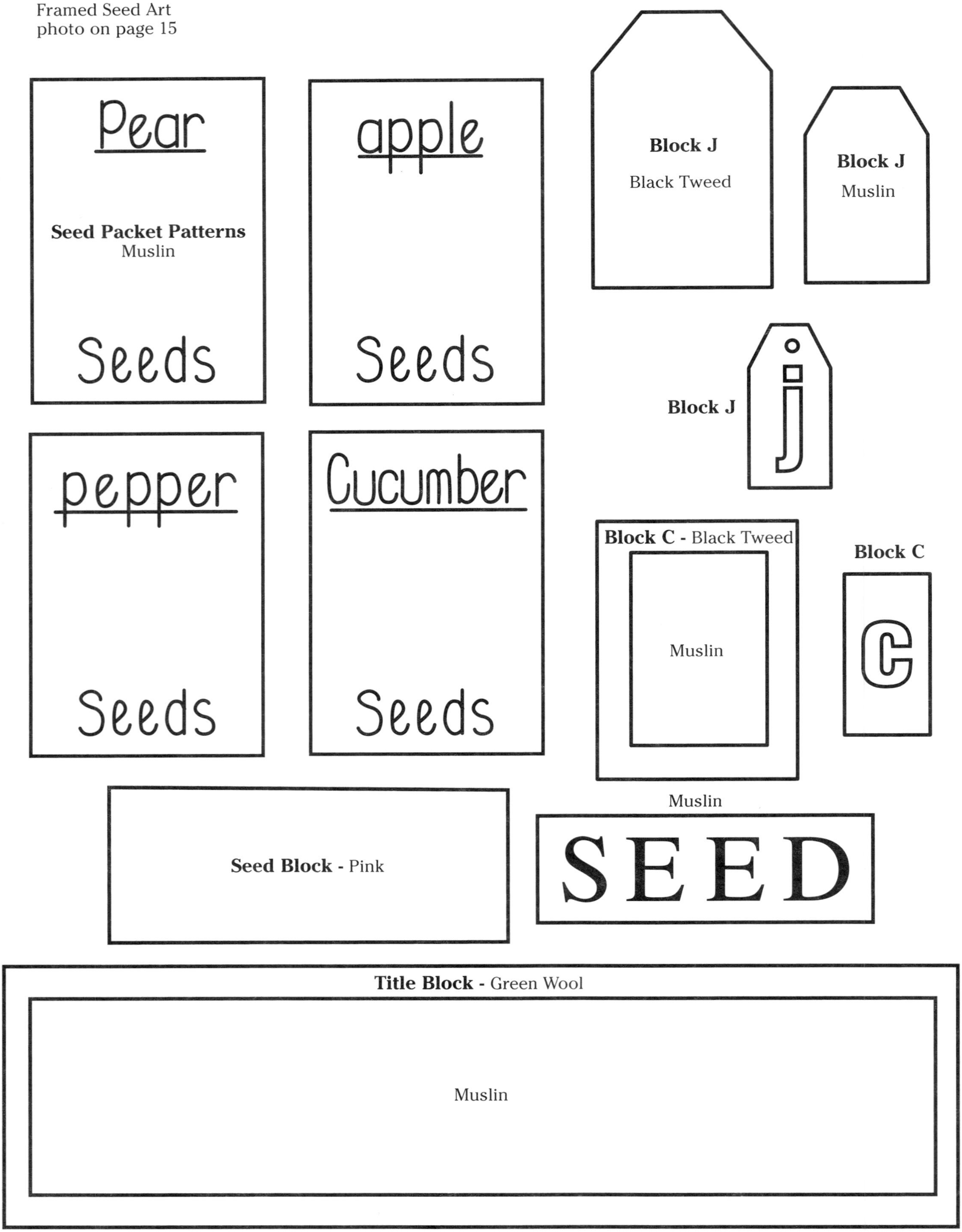

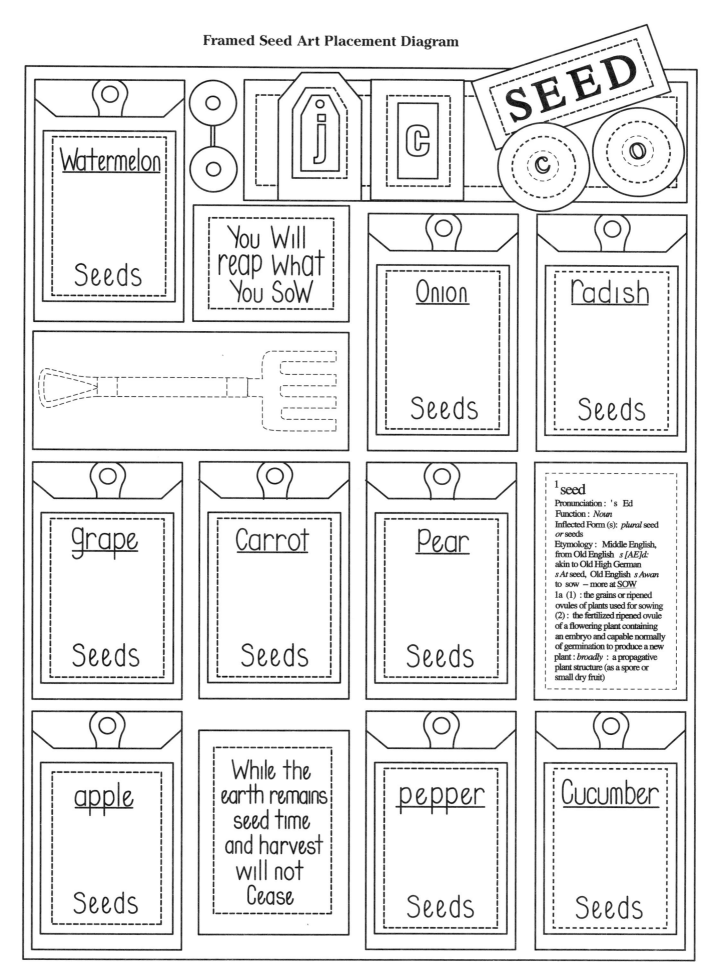

SEED

Watermelon

Seeds

You Will reap What You SoW

Onion

Seeds

radish

Seeds

Grape

Seeds

Carrot

Seeds

Pear

Seeds

¹ seed
Pronunciation : 's Ed
Function : *Noun*
Inflected Form (s): *plural* seed
or seeds
Etymology : Middle English,
from Old English *s [AE]d:*
akin to Old High German
s At seed, Old English *s Awan*
to sow – more at SOW
1a (1) : the grains or ripened
ovules of plants used for sowing
(2) : the fertilized ripened ovule
of a flowering plant containing
an embryo and capable normally
of germination to produce a new
plant : *broadly* : a propagative
plant structure (as a spore or
small dry fruit)

apple

Seeds

While the
earth remains
seed time
and harvest
will not
Cease

pepper

Seeds

Cucumber

Seeds

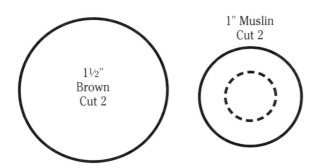

1½"
Brown
Cut 2

1" Muslin
Cut 2

Rust

You Will
reap What
You SoW

Muslin

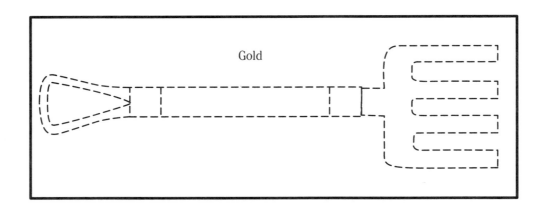

Gold

Seed Definition
Houndstooth Suiting

[1]seed

Pronunciation : 's Ed
Function : *Noun*
Inflected Form (s): *plural* seed
or seeds
Etymology : Middle English,
from Old English s [AE]d:
akin to Old High German
s At seed, Old English *s Awan*
to sow -- more at SOW
1a (1) : the grains or ripened
ovules of plants used for sowing
(2) : the fertilized ripened ovule
of a flowering plant containing
an embryo and capable normally
of germination to produce a new
plant : *broadly* : a propagative
plant structure (as a spore or
small dry fruit)

Tan Cardstock

Gold Seed Packets
Cut 9

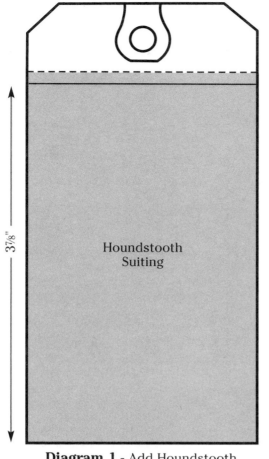

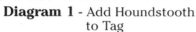

37⁄8"

Houndstooth
Suiting

Diagram 1 - Add Houndstooth
to Tag

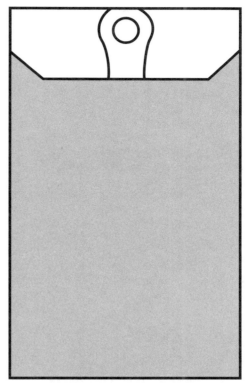

Diagram 2 - Tag Closed

While the Earth Remains -
Gold

While the
earth remains
seed time
and harvest
will not
Cease

Muslin

Seed Art Border Diagram

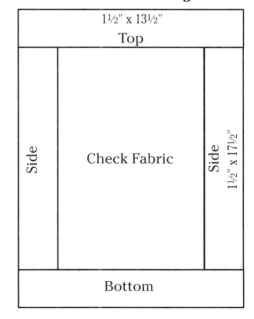

1½" x 13½"
Top

Side

Check Fabric

Side

1½" x 17½"

Bottom

Pumpkin Purse and Pumpkin Harvest Journal
photo on pages 16 and 17

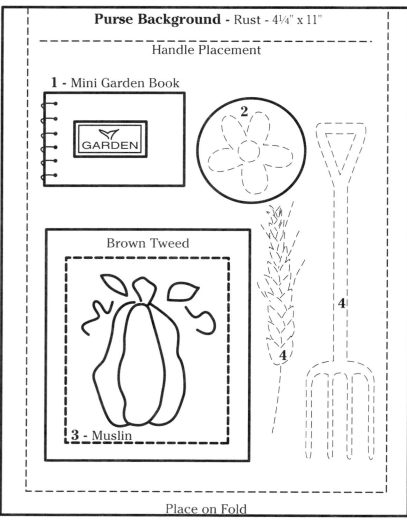

Purse Background - Rust - 4¼" x 11"

Handle Placement

1 - Mini Garden Book

GARDEN

2

Brown Tweed

4

4

3 - Muslin

Place on Fold

Pumpkin Purse

MATERIALS:
Wool (4¼" x 11" Rust, 2⅛" x 2½" Brown Tweed, 1¼" x 3" Tan) • 1½" x 2" Muslin • *Jolee's By You* assorted embellishments • Markers (Black, Orange, Green) • *DMC* floss (Tan, Brown, Dark Brown) • Needle • Thread • E6000

INSTRUCTIONS:
See General Instructions on page 20. Follow steps 1-8.

Block 1: Adhere mini garden book.

Block 2: Blanket stitch a 1" circle of Tan wool to the purse with Brown floss. • Adhere Yellow flower.

Block 3: Draw a pumpkin on the muslin. Backstitch pumpkin lines with Brown floss, leaves and stem with Green floss. • Color the pumpkin with markers. • Blanket stitch Muslin to the Tweed with Dark Brown floss. Blanket stitch Tweed to purse with Tan floss.

Block 4: Adhere the wheat stalk and pitch fork to purse.

Continue with Step 9 of the General Instructions on page 20.

Pumpkin Harvest Journal
Placement Diagram
photo on pages 16 and 17

harvest

Cut 1

Cut 5

Grape Patterns

pear

Purse & Journal
Pattern

SEEDS

Pumpkin Harvest Journal

MATERIALS:

Wool (9" x 23" Plaid cover, 5" x 6¾" Brown/White Tweed, 5⅛" x 6" Gray Plaid, 2½" x 4" Brown, ⅝" x 6¼" Tan) • Wool appliques (1⅝" x 3" Light Brown for Pear, 1⅞" x 2" Gold for grapes, 1⅞" x 2½" Dark Brown for pumpkin, 3" scrap Purple for grapes, 3" scrap Green for pear) • Muslin (1½" x 2" for pumpkin; ¾" x 2¼" for harvest) • *ColorBox* ink (Chestnut Roan, Dark Green) • Pigma pen (Orange, Green, Black) • 3 Orange buttons • Trowel charm • 1½" x 3" Shipping tag • 4 small Brown brads • *DMC* floss (Brown, Dark Green, Purple, Pink, Dark Brown, Tan, Black, Gold) • Needle • Thread • Steam-A-Seam II

INSTRUCTIONS:

1. Transfer vine pattern to Tan wool strip. Embroider flowers with 4 Purple French Knots, 1 Gold French Knot in the center, and Backstitch a vine with Dark Green floss.

2. Apply Steam-A-Seam II to all pieces 1-4. Position according to Wool Placement Diagram below. Press in place.

3. Blanket stitch around #3 with Brown floss, and around #4 with Pink floss.

4. Cut out wool applique rectangles. Apply Steam-A-Seam II.

5. Trace grapes, stem, and pear onto Steam-A-Seam II. Apply to fabric. Cut out pieces.

6. **Pear block**: Fuse Pear to Light Brown wool. Backstitch "Pear" word and Blanket stitch the Pear applique with Dark Green floss. Fuse to background. Blanket stitch around with Dark Brown floss. Insert brads.

7. **Grapes block**: Fuse Grapes and stem to Gold wool. Fuse Gold wool in place. Blanket stitch around with Dark Brown floss.

8. **Pumpkin block**: Trace pumpkin pattern onto Muslin with Black pigma pen. Color. Embroider pumpkin with Brown floss, leaves with Dark Green floss. Apply Steam-A-Seam II to the back of the Muslin. Ink the edges with Chestnut Roan. Fuse to Dark Brown wool. Blanket stitch around the Muslin with Dark Brown floss. Fuse to the background. Blanket stitch around wool with Tan floss.

9. **Harvest block**: Draw the oval and word onto Muslin. Backstitch words with Dark Brown floss. Cut out oval. Apply Steam-A-Seam II. Ink the edges with Chestnut Roan and Green. Fuse to background. Blanket stitch with Dark Green floss.

10. **Tag block**: Transfer pattern and "seeds" to shipping tag. Ink the edges with Chestnut Roan and Green. Apply Steam-A-Seam II. Fuse to background. Blanket stitch around the tag with Dark Brown floss. Satin stitch at the top of the hole with Black floss. Sew the trowel charm in place.

11. Sew 3 buttons in place with Tan floss.

12. Make the book cover following the General Instructions on page 19.

13. Fuse to book cover. Blanket stitch around the Background with Tan floss.

Pumpkin Harvest Journal Placement Patterns

Vine Pattern

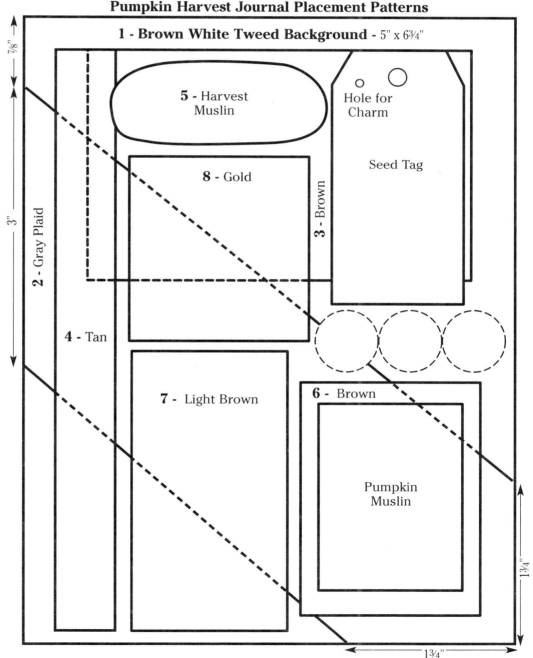

Harvest Journal
photo on page 16

Harvest Journal

MATERIALS:
Muslin 9" x 23" cover
• *Design Originals* 3 Silver bottle caps • Three 1" buttons • *ColorBox* ink (Pink, Dark Green) • *DMC* floss (Dark Green, Medium Green, Red, Coral, Burgundy, Yellow) • Needle • Thread • Rubber mallet • Hammer • Small nail

INSTRUCTIONS:
1. Make the book cover following the General Instructions below.
2. See Placement Diagram to transfer words and stems to Muslin. Backstitch words with Dark Green and Red. Backstitch stems in Medium Green.
3. Punch a hole in the center of each bottle cap with a small nail. Place a button in each bottle cap and flatten the flange around with a rubber mallet.
4. Sew bottle caps to cover with Coral, Burgundy, and Yellow floss.

Making the Soft Book Cover

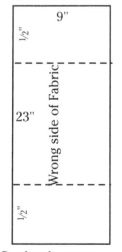

1. Cut book cover.

the harvest you
gather tomorrow
are the Seeds you Plant today

Sow Seeds of
Kindness • truth • Endurance
and you will grow
friendship • Wisdom • Strength

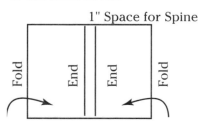

2. Fold cover ends in 5½".

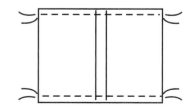

3. Sew across long ends. Trim threads and turn cover right side out.

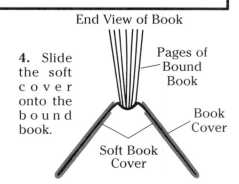

4. Slide the soft cover onto the bound book.

Red

Red

Red

Red

Red

Green

Muslin

Home: where my flowers grow

Red

Green

Tan

Tan

Yellow

Bloom Where You Are Planted!

1" x 11 1/8" - Olive Green

Garden
Blooms
Wall Quilt
photo on
page 18

Gold Circles
for Flowers

B L O O O M

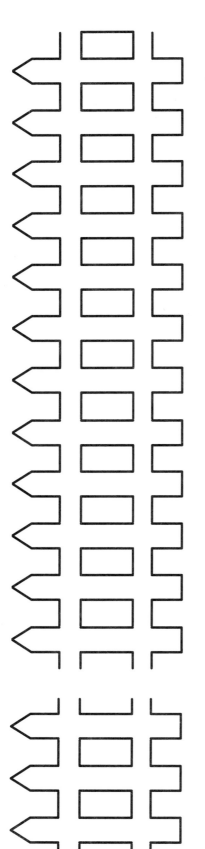

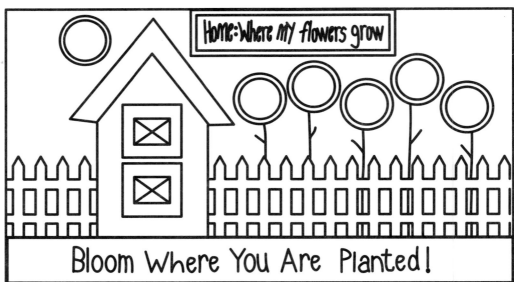

Garden Blooms Placement Diagram

Garden Blooms Wall Quilt

FINISHED SIZE:
9¼" x 14"

MATERIALS:
¼ yard Beige wool for center
⅛ yard Olive Green wool for bottom strip and applique
⅓ yard Tan wool for backing and windows
⅛ yard Green print for outer border

CUTTING:
Cut Center
1   9" x 18" from Beige
1   1" x 12" from Olive Green
Cut Border strips
2 strips   1½" x 7" for sides
2 strips   1½ " x 14" for top and bottom

BACKING AND BATTING
1   9¼" x 14"

WOOL APPLIQUE:
 (2" x 11" Brown Tweed, 1" square Yellow, 2" x 3" Gold, 3" x 4" Red) • 1" x 5" Muslin • *DMC* floss (Ecru, Red, Light Brown, Brown, Gray, Dark Green, Light Green) • *DMC* Red Pearl Cotton #5 • *Design Originals* 6 Silver bottle caps • Steam-A-Seam II • Warm & Natural cotton batting • E6000

INSTRUCTIONS:

1. Write "Bloom Where You Are Planted!" onto the bottom Olive Green strip and Backstitch with Red pearl cotton.
2. Use Steam-A-Seam II to fuse the Olive Green strip in place.
    The bottom of the strip is 1¼" from the bottom of the center piece.
3. Fuse the side borders and top/bottom borders in place.
4. Blanket stitch around the inside borders and across the upper edge of the bottom Olive strip with Light Green floss.

APPLIQUE:

5. Trace all of the applique pieces onto the fusible web paper using a light table.
6. Using the picture as a color guide, press the fusible web pieces to the appropriate fabrics.
7. Cut out shapes.
8. Write "Home: where my flowers grow" on Muslin and Backstitch with Red floss.
9. Position pieces and fuse in place.

EMBROIDERY:

10. Sew a Running stitch with Brown floss, around all of the fence.
11. Blanket stitch around windows with Ecru floss.
12. Backstitch the interior rectangles with Light Brown floss.
13. Blanket stitch around roof, the top edge of the grass, and the Green rectangle with Light Green floss.
14. Blanket stitch around Muslin rectangle with Gray.
15. Backstitch words with Red floss.
16. Draw the flower stems and Backstitch with Dark Green floss.

FINISHING:

17. Layer backing, batting and top.
18. Blanket stitch all around the edge.

BOTTLE CAPS:

19. Flatten 6 bottle caps.
20. Blanket stitch around the Yellow circle with Gray floss.
21. Cut 5 Red and 5 Gold circles using pattern.
22. Fuse Gold circles to the Red.
23. Blanket stitch around the edges with Dark Green floss.
24. Embroider letters with Red pearl cotton.
25. Adhere circles to the bottle caps with E6000.
26. Adhere bottle caps to top of flower stems with E6000.

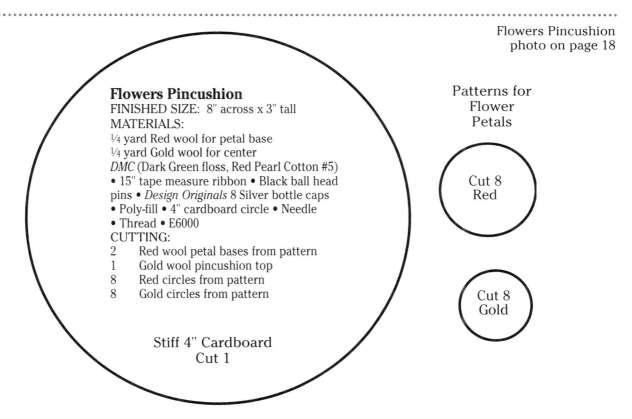

Flowers Pincushion
FINISHED SIZE: 8" across x 3" tall
MATERIALS:
¼ yard Red wool for petal base
¼ yard Gold wool for center
DMC (Dark Green floss, Red Pearl Cotton #5)
• 15" tape measure ribbon • Black ball head pins • *Design Originals* 8 Silver bottle caps
• Poly-fill • 4" cardboard circle • Needle
• Thread • E6000
CUTTING:
2   Red wool petal bases from pattern
1   Gold wool pincushion top
8   Red circles from pattern
8   Gold circles from pattern

Stiff 4" Cardboard
Cut 1

Patterns for
Flower
Petals

Cut 8
Red

Cut 8
Gold

INSTRUCTIONS:

1. In Gold top, sew darts closed.
2. Sew a Gather stitch ¼" from the bottom edge.
3. Turn right side out and stuff.
4. Place the cardboard circle over the stuffing. Add more stuffing until the pincushion is very firm.
5. Pull gather threads just enough to wrap the fabric around the edge of the cardboard.
6. Tie a secure knot.

BASE:

7. Place Red petal base pieces together.
Blanket stitch around the edges with Green floss.

ASSEMBLY:

8. Place Gold top in the center of the petals.
9. Pin and Whipstitch in place.
10. Wrap the tape measure ribbon as in photo.
11. Pin tape measure in place.

BOTTLE CAPS:

12. Flatten 8 bottle caps.
13. Blanket stitch the Red and Gold circles together.
14. Draw the letters on the Gold circles.
15. Backstitch letters with Red pearl cotton.
16. Adhere circles to the bottle caps with E6000.
17. Adhere bottle caps in place with E6000.

Flowers Pincushion continued on pages 60 and 61

Flowers Pincushion
photo on page 18

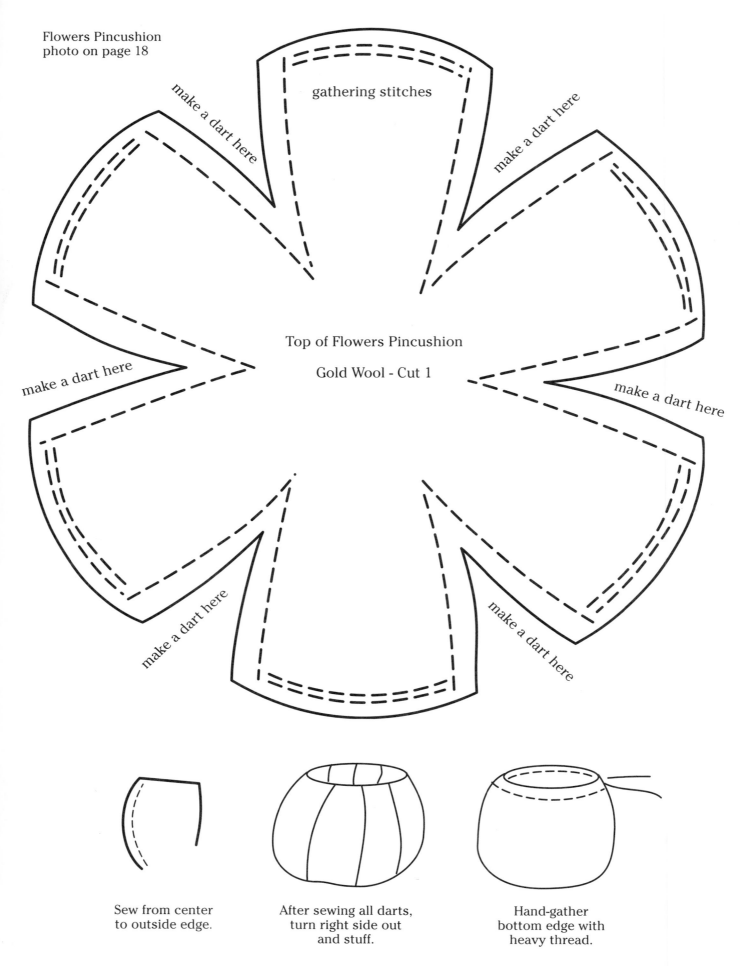

make a dart here

gathering stitches

make a dart here

make a dart here

make a dart here

Top of Flowers Pincushion

Gold Wool - Cut 1

make a dart here

make a dart here

make a dart here

Sew from center
to outside edge.

After sewing all darts,
turn right side out
and stuff.

Hand-gather
bottom edge with
heavy thread.

Flowers Pin Cushion
photo on page 18

Petal Base
Cut 2
Red Wool

Embroidery Patterns
for Gold Circles

Sewing Purse
photo on page 67

Purse Patterns and Placement Diagram

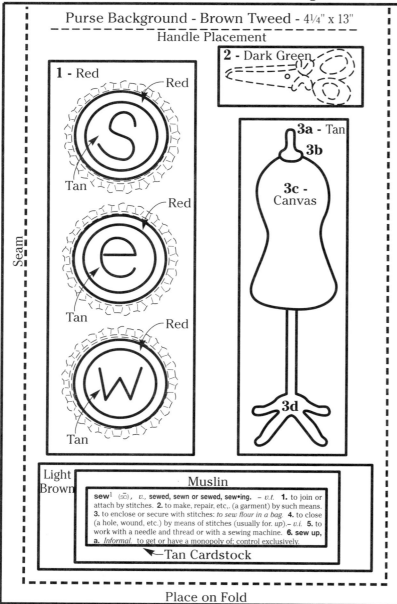

Purse Background - Brown Tweed - 4¼" x 13"

Handle Placement

2 - Dark Green

1 - Red

Red

S

Tan

Red

e

Tan

Red

W

Tan

3a - Tan

3b

3c - Canvas

3d

Seam

Light Brown

Muslin

sew¹ (sō), *v.*, sewed, sewn or sewed, sew•ing. – *v.t.* **1.** to join or attach by stitches. **2.** to make, repair, etc,. (a garment) by such means. **3.** to enclose or secure with stitches: *to sew flour in a bag.* **4.** to close (a hole, wound, etc.) by means of stitches (usually for. *up*).– *v.i.* **5.** to work with a needle and thread or with a sewing machine. **6. sew up, a.** *Informal.* to get or have a monopoly of; control exclusively.

←Tan Cardstock

Place on Fold

Every dressmaker needs a scissors fob. This purse will hang around your neck and to store your scissors and other accents.

Sewing Purse
MATERIALS:
Wool (4¼" x 13" Brown Tweed, 1½" x 4½" Red, 1⅛" x 3⅝" Tan, ⅝" x 1½" Dark Green, 1¼" x 3⅝" Light Brown) • 1" x 2" canvas • 1" x 2¾" Muslin • *Design Originals* 3 Silver bottle caps • Cardstock (Tan, Dark Brown) • *Jolee's By You* scissors charm • *DMC* floss (Light Green, Brown, Dark Green) • Needle • Thread • Small nail • Hammer • Rubber mallet • Steam-A-Seam II • E6000
INSTRUCTIONS:
Follow General Instructions for steps 1-8 on page 20.
Block 1: Blanket stitch the Red wool in place with Light Green floss. • Flatten 3 bottle caps. Punch 2 holes in each cap. Sew caps in place. • Cut out Red and Tan wool circles using the pattern. • Embroider the letters with Dark Green floss. • Blanket stitch the Tan circle to the Red circle with Dark Green floss. Adhere the circles to the caps with E6000.
Block 2: Blanket stitch the Dark Green wool to the purse with Light Green floss. • Sew the scissors charm in place.
Block 3: Blanket stitch the Tan wool to the purse with Brown floss. • Trace the reverse pattern of 3c onto Steam-A-Seam II. Cut out and press to canvas. Cut out canvas dress form and press in place. • Cut out 3b and 3d from Dark Brown cardstock. Adhere in place with E6000.
Block 4: Blanket stitch Muslin to Light Brown wool with Brown floss. • Blanket stitch Light Brown wool to purse with Light Green floss. • Copy definition onto Tan cardstock. Adhere dictionary definition to Muslin. Continue General Instructions with Step 9 on page 20.

Dictionary Definition

sew¹ (sō), *v.*, sewed, sewn or sewed, sew•ing. – *v.t.* **1.** to join or attach by stitches. **2.** to make, repair, etc,. (a garment) by such means. **3.** to enclose or secure with stitches: *to sew flour in a bag.* **4.** to close (a hole, wound, etc.) by means of stitches (usually for. *up*).– *v.i.* **5.** to work with a needle and thread or with a sewing machine. **6. sew up, a.** *Informal.* to get or have a monopoly of; control exclusively.

For Boxes: Cut ⅞" circles from Ecru. Backstitch letters in Dark Green Floss.

Tomato Pincushion
Patterns
photo on page 67
instructions on page 63

Thread Box
Patterns
photo page 67
instructions
on page 63

Button Box
Patterns
photo
p. 67
inst.
on p. 63

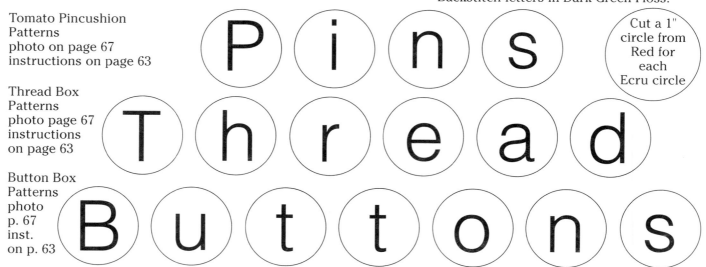

P i n s

Cut a 1" circle from Red for each Ecru circle

T h r e a d

B u t t o n s

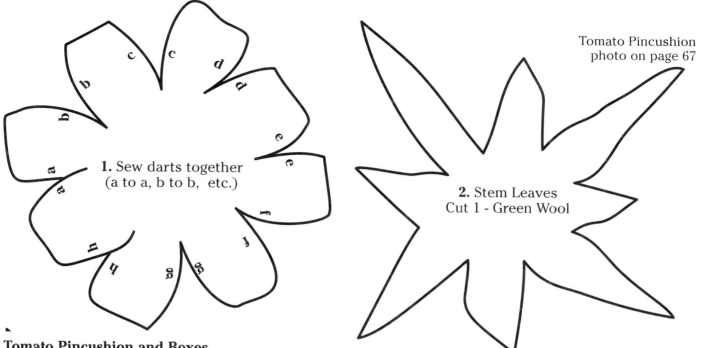

1. Sew darts together
(a to a, b to b, etc.)

Tomato Pincushion
photo on page 67

2. Stem Leaves
Cut 1 - Green Wool

Tomato Pincushion and Boxes

Turn an ordinary box into something special with an embroidered label made of bottle caps and circles of wool. Reminiscent of the old style penny rugs, these boxes will become collectibles.

FINISHED SIZE: 3"x 4½" x 5½"

MATERIALS FOR PINCUSHION:
½ yard Red wool (14" x 14" piece)
⅛ yard Dark Green wool
Poly-fill stuffing • *DMC* Dark Green pearl cotton #5 • Upholstery Needle • Strong thread
MATERIALS FOR BOXES:
3 nested paper mache boxes (2" x 4" x 5¼"; 2¼" x 4½" x 5¾"; 2½" x 5" x 6¼")
• 4" square wool (Ecru, Red) • *DMC* Dark Green floss • *Design Originals* 17 Silver bottle caps • 16" tape measure • Small brass brad • Steam-A-Seam II • E6000

Tomato Pincushion

INSTRUCTIONS:

1. Cut 1 on double fold from Red wool. Draw vines from pattern. See page 64.
2. Open. Embroider the vines with 6 strands of Green floss.
3. Sew the darts. See Diagram 1 above.
4. After sewing all darts, turn right-side-out and stuff. It will look large. See Diagram 3 at right.
5. Hand-gather the bottom edge with strong thread. Pull thread tight and knot it. See Diagram 4.
6. To crease the tomato, use a long piece of strong Red thread and a long needle.
7. Push the needle through the top center. Go straight down through the center bottom.
8. Bring thread over a seam, and push the needle down through the center top and through the center bottom.
9. Pull thread tight. Repeat for all 8 seams.
10. Tie and knot the thread.
11. Tack stitch stem leaves to top center of tomato.
12. Put tomato cushion into the small box. It will fit tightly.

Boxes

INSTRUCTIONS:

1. Cut out larger circles from Red wool
2. Cut out and Steam-A-Seam II smaller Ecru circles.
3. Transfer letters onto small circles.
4. Blanket stitch around all with Green floss.
5. Backstitch letters with Dark Green floss.
6. Glue centers onto caps. Let dry completely.
7. Flatten bottle caps.
8. Line up bottle caps on the front center of boxes.

3. After sewing all seams, turn right-side-out and stuff.

4. Hand gather bottom edge with strong thread.

5. Top view with vine stitching.

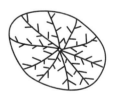

CUTTING:
1   Red wool tomato from pattern
1   Green wool pincushion top
17   Red circles from pattern
17   Gold circles from pattern

9. Start with the 2 center caps, about ½" up from bottom edge.
10. Glue all caps on the boxes with E6000 glue.

Tip: You will need to lay the box on its side and glue only 1 or 2 caps at a time to allow glue to dry enough to hold the caps in place.

Blanket Stitch

Backstitch

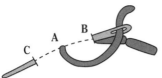

Come up at A, go down at B. Come back up at C. Repeat.

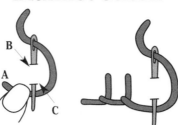

Come up at A, hold the thread down with your thumb, go down at B. Come back up at C with the needle tip over the thread. Pull the stitch into place. Repeat, outlining with the bottom legs of the stitch. Use this stitch to edge fabrics.

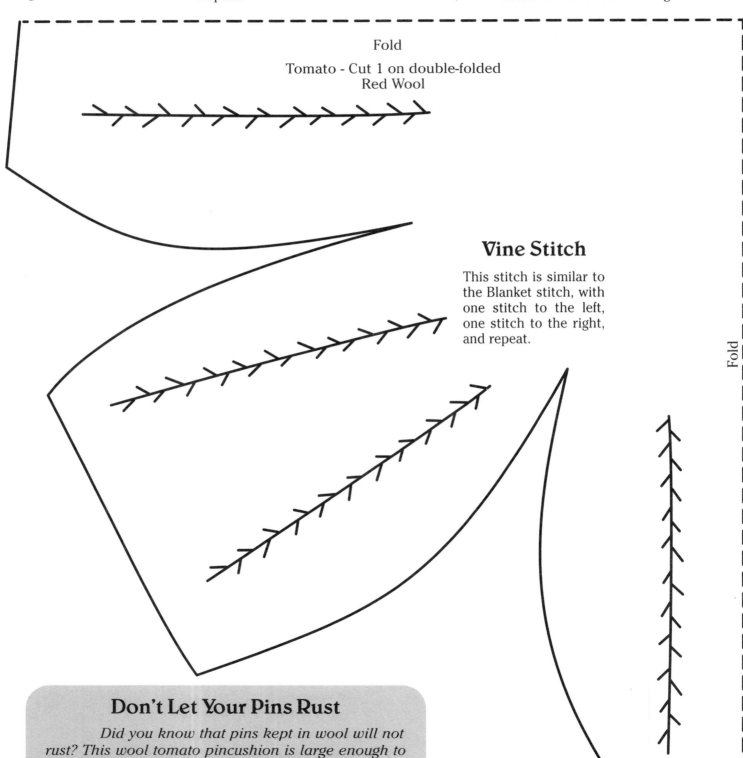

Fold

Tomato - Cut 1 on double-folded
Red Wool

Fold

Vine Stitch

This stitch is similar to the Blanket stitch, with one stitch to the left, one stitch to the right, and repeat.

Don't Let Your Pins Rust

Did you know that pins kept in wool will not rust? This wool tomato pincushion is large enough to accommodate the big pins used by quilters.

Sewing Wall Quilt

This small hanging has everything a seamstress needs: scissors, buttons, tomato pincushion, and fabric swatches. Make the title with wool circles and bottle caps.

FINISHED SIZE: 6¼" x 8¼"

MATERIALS:
¼ yard Brown Tweed for center
¼ yard Light Green for backing, borders and applique
⅛ yard Gold
Wool Appliques (4" x 5" Gold; 2" x 6" Medium Green, 2" x 2" Rust, 2" x 3" Red, 3" x 3" Black Tan Houndstooth, 2" x 2' Dark Green, 3" x 5" Navy Tan Houndstooth, 2" x 2" Black Brown Tweed, 2" squares of Tan, Lavender, Dark Rose) • 1" square Muslin • *DMC floss (Dark Green, Tan, Black, Gray)* • *Design Originals* 4 Silver bottle caps • Scissors charm • 4 tiny Red buttons • 2 clear 11° seed beads • Steam-A-Seam II • E6000

CUTTING:
Cut Brown Tweed Background
1   6¼" x 8¼"
Cut Light Green Backing
1   6¼" x 8¼"
Cut out Light Green Borders
2 strips   ¾" x 8¼" for sides
2 strips   ¾" x 5¼" for top and bottom
WOOL PLACEMENT:
For #1: 2⅛" x 4½" Gold
For #2: 1⅛" x 2⅛" Medium Green
For #3: 2¼" x 2¾" Light Green
For #4: 1½" x 1⅝" Rust
For #5: 1¼" x 2⅜" Gold
WOOL FOR BLOCKS:
For #1: 3 Light Green ¾" circles, 3 Red 1" circles, 1 Black/Tan Houndstooth 2" circle, 1 Green tag, 1¾" x 4¼" Navy/Tan Houndstooth rectangle
For #2: ¾" x 1¾" Black/Brown Tweed, ⅝" x ⅞" Muslin
For #3: 1" x 1½" from each color: Black/Brown Tweed, Tan, Medium Green, Lavender, Light Green, Dark Rose
For #4: Red tomato, Medium Green stem
For #5: 1" x 1⅞" Medium Green

INSTRUCTIONS:
BACKGROUND & BORDERS:
1. Apply Steam-A-Seam II to the border strips.
2. Position top and bottom border pieces on background.
3. Position right and left border pieces on background.
4. Press pieces together.
5. Blanket stitch around the inside of the border with Gray floss.
BLOCKS:
6. Press all pieces onto Steam-A-Seam II.
7. Flatten 4 bottle caps.
8. **Block 1**: Draw the letters "s", "e", and "w" on the small Tan circles. Fuse to the Red circles. Blanket stitch around the Light Green circles with Dark Green floss. Backstitch the letters with Dark Green floss. Adhere circles to bottle caps with E6000. Set aside and let dry. Fuse the Navy/Tan Houndstooth rectangle in place. Blanket stitch with Tan floss. Fuse the Green tag and Blanket stitch in place with

Sewing Wall Quilt Placement Diagram

Dark Green floss. Fuse the Houndstooth circle in place. Blanket stitch around with Tan floss.

9. **Block 2**: Fuse Tweed rectangle in place. Blanket stitch with Tan floss. Fuse the Muslin in place. Blanket stitch with Tan floss. Sew the Red buttons in place with Tan floss. Print the word "Buttons" to fit on ¼" x ½" Manila cardstock. Cut out. Apply Steam-A-Seam II to the back. Fuse in place.

10. **Block 3**: Fuse the rectangles in place. Blanket stitch with Dark Green floss.

11. **Block 4**: Trace tomato pincushion patterns onto Steam-A-Seam II. Fuse to fabrics. Cut out. Fuse Green top to Red pincushion. Embroider the lines with 1 strand of Gray floss, adding beads to look like pin heads. Adhere to a bottle cap with E6000. Set aside and let dry.

12. **Block 5**: Fuse the rectangle in place. Blanket stitch with Tan floss. Sew the scissors charm in place.

FINISHING:
13. Position the backing.
14. Blanket stitch around the outside border edge with Gray floss.
15. Adhere bottle caps in place with E6000. Let dry.

Sewing Wall Quilt continued on page 66

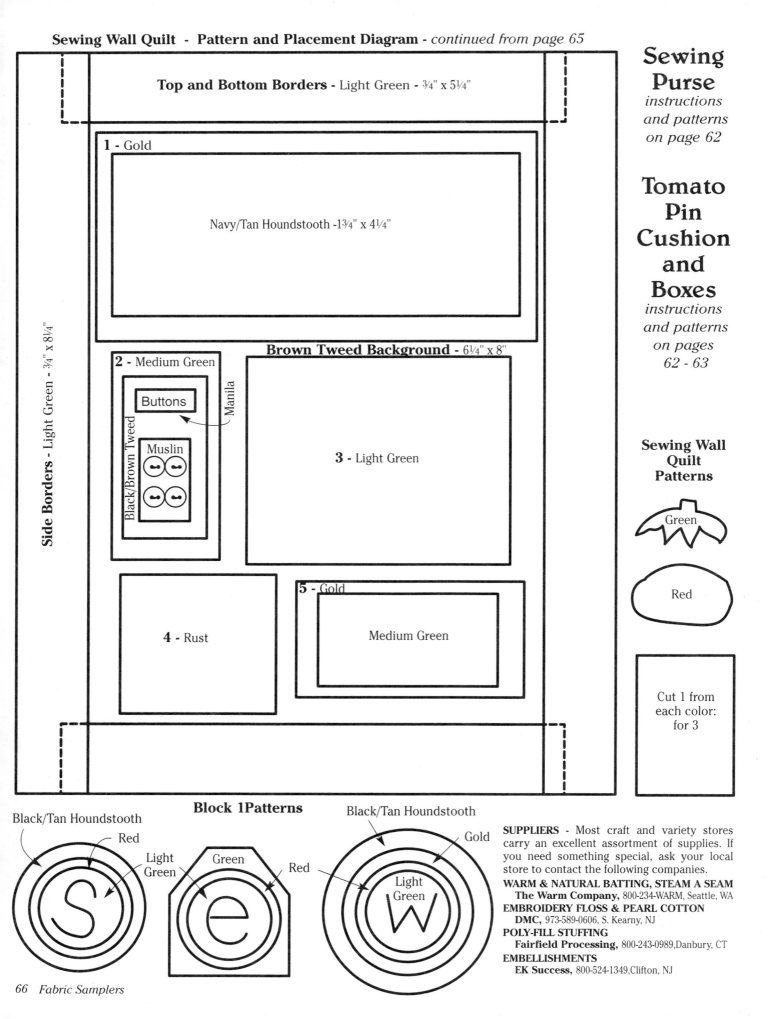

Top and Bottom Borders - Light Green - ¾" x 5¼"

1 - Gold

Navy/Tan Houndstooth -1¾" x 4¼"

Side Borders - Light Green - ¾" x 8¼"

2 - Medium Green

Black/Brown Tweed

Manila

Buttons

Muslin

Brown Tweed Background - 6¼" x 8"

3 - Light Green

4 - Rust

5 - Gold

Medium Green

Sewing Purse *instructions and patterns on page 62*

Tomato Pin Cushion and Boxes *instructions and patterns on pages 62 - 63*

Sewing Wall Quilt Patterns

Green

Red

Cut 1 from each color: for 3

Block 1 Patterns

Black/Tan Houndstooth

Red

Light Green

Green

Red

Black/Tan Houndstooth

Gold

Light Green

SUPPLIERS - Most craft and variety stores carry an excellent assortment of supplies. If you need something special, ask your local store to contact the following companies.

WARM & NATURAL BATTING, STEAM A SEAM
The Warm Company, 800-234-WARM, Seattle, WA

EMBROIDERY FLOSS & PEARL COTTON
DMC, 973-589-0606, S. Kearny, NJ

POLY-FILL STUFFING
Fairfield Processing, 800-243-0989, Danbury, CT

EMBELLISHMENTS
EK Success, 800-524-1349, Clifton, NJ